THE ENRAGED
ACCOMPANIST'S GUIDE
TO THE PERFECT AUDITION

Praise for Andrew Gerle's
The Enraged Accompanist's Guide to the Perfect Audition

"Andrew Gerle's book is just astonishingly good. It is funny, it is complete, and so practical. Any performer who has ever faced, or plans to face, the mystical and terrifying experience called 'the audition' will find out how to maneuver through it, be better at it, and actually enjoy it. Andrew's style is laugh-out-loud entertaining, but underneath, this book seriously tells you how you can remain the artist you set out to be while enduring a process that seems designed only to humiliate. Read this book. You'll be a better and happier performer, you'll understand what is going on, and you'll get more jobs. What more could you ask for?"

—Richard Maltby, Jr., American theatre director and producer, lyricist, and screenwriter

"How did he get inside my head??? All my crazy actress fears, insecurities and questions are voiced and answered in this hilarious and informative book. I wish it had been around when I was in drama school. It would have saved me a lot of guesswork and a whole lot of tears. From the seemingly smallest detail (how to Xerox your music/why plastic sheet covers suck) to the really meaty stuff (how to act a lyric), Gerle tells it like it is with wit, years of first hand experience, and perhaps most importantly, joy. Since reading this book, I have embraced and enjoyed auditioning, and have increased my callbacks and bookings substantially. His words have given me freedom and joy in the audition room. How lucky we are to be actors, singers, and dancers! And how lucky we are to have this book and Andrew to help us along the way."

—Piper Goodeve, Drama League Award nominee, professional auditioner

"Andrew Gerle writes from the unique perspective of someone both performing in an audition and hearing the comments afterwards. In his invaluable book, not only does he advise brilliantly on the technical aspects of preparing and performing a good musical audition, but he goes beyond technique into the even more important aspects of how to reveal the unique aspects of your talent and relax into being yourself in this stressful situation.

I found myself laughing and nodding in agreement with something on every page. Mr. Gerle writes with a sympathetic tone and an acid wit. His understanding of what directors and music directors look for in auditions is spot on . . . I recommend this book to anyone auditioning today."

—Ted Sperling, Tony Award–winning musical director and orchestrator

"This book takes the mystery out of the audition process. Written with great wisdom, insight, and humor, Gerle gives a master class on the art of the singing audition. There's something here for all singers—from the kid getting out of school to the seasoned pro—miss it at your own peril. This book is indispensable for anyone who wants to land a job in the musical theatre."

—Deborah Lapidus, faculty at Juilliard Drama and Associate Professor at NYU Tisch Graduate Acting

"If you have ever auditioned for the musical theater or ever plan to audition you must read this book! Andrew Gerle's love of craft and talent has overcome his accompanist's rage at the lack of understanding of what it takes to successfully audition and he is ready to help you. Where was he when I needed him? Oh . . . not yet born . . . Well, he is here for you! Break a leg!"

—Mark Linn-Baker, actor and director

THE ENRAGED
ACCOMPANIST'S GUIDE
TO THE PERFECT AUDITION

Andrew Gerle

APPLAUSE
THEATRE & CINEMA BOOKS

An Imprint of
Hal Leonard Corporation

Copyright © 2011 by Andrew Gerle

Published in 2011 by Applause Theatre & Cinema Books
An Imprint of Hal Leonard Corporation
7777 West Bluemound Road
Milwaukee, WI 53213

Trade Book Division Editorial Offices
33 Plymouth St., Montclair, NJ 07042

Printed in the United States of America

Book design by Lynn Bergesen
Illustrations by Cliff Mott

Lyrics permissions can be found on page 113, which constitute an extension of this copyright page.

Library of Congress Cataloging-in-Publication Data

Gerle, Andrew.
   The enraged accompanist's guide to the perfect audition / Andrew Gerle.
   p. cm.
Includes index.
ISBN 978-1-4234-9705-9 (pbk.)
   1. Musicals—Auditions. 2. Singing—Auditions. I. Title.
MT956.G47 2011
783'.04—dc22
                                          2010051027

www.applausepub.com

for my parents, who taught me how to teach

CONTENTS

CHAPTER 1

Who Am I? • *page 1*

CHAPTER 2

What Is an Audition?
(And What Is It Not?) • *page 7*

CHAPTER 3

What Are They Looking For? • *page 17*

CHAPTER 4

Your Book • *page 23*

The Music – 23
The Index – 31

CHAPTER 5

Nuts and Bolts:
Everything but the Singing • *page 35*

In the Room – 35
Before You Arrive – 40
The Ultimate Mystery: What Do I Wear? – 41

CHAPTER 6

How to Talk to Me • *page 47*

CHAPTER 7

The Song • *page 55*

CHAPTER 8

How to Sing It—Part I:
Interpretation • *page 65*

CHAPTER 9

How to Sing It—Part II:
Audition Technique • *page 79*

Sides – *79*
Technique and Staging – *81*
Practicing Your Audition – *85*

CHAPTER 10

Headshots and Résumés • *page 91*

Your Headshot – *91*
Your Résumé – *94*

CHAPTER 11

Who Are You? • *page 99*

APPENDIX

Four-by-Four: In a Nutshell • *page 107*

General Audition To-Do List – *107*
The Day Before To-Do List – *109*
At the Audition To-Do List – *110*
After the Call To-Do List – *111*

THE ENRAGED ACCOMPANIST'S GUIDE
TO THE PERFECT AUDITION

1

WHO AM I?

I am your accompanist. You do not know me. I am the guy who sits behind the upright in the unflattering fluorescent light of the dance studio, a bottle of water on the floor, a half-eaten Power Bar on the bench, and your audition in my hands.

My job can be a joy. Accompanying talented strangers, crafting a nuanced performance after only a ten-second conference can feel like magic. Rocking out a great song with a responsive, musical singer, trying something a little different and having them go with me (and vice versa) is a thrill akin to the hottest of blind dates.

But usually it sucks.

Playing from music that is badly prepared makes me enraged. You try reading illegible faxes and fighting the Amazing Self-Closing Book two hundred times a day. Playing bad songs makes me enraged. No tune, no money note, no joke, no point. Idiotic sixteen-bar versions of great songs make me enraged. Death by a thousand bad cuts. Playing the same song over and over and over makes me enraged. Trying to read the minds of singers who have never been taught how to talk to a pianist makes me enraged. "What tempo do you like?" "I don't know." "You don't *know?*" "Whatever it says." Shoot me.

But the thing that makes me the most enraged, the thing that makes me want to stop the audition and stand up on the piano bench, stomp my feet, and throw an eighty-five-pound glitter- and decal-encrusted binder across the room is seeing actors with the potential to knock an audition out of the park give yet another ho-hum, serenely competent, comfortable, "Who's next?" performance and watching them walk out the door, knowing they think they did a great job, knowing they won't get a callback, and knowing they'll give the same audition every day for the next five years (if they last that long) and never be remembered.

They can do better. A lot better. And I know how.

I am your partner, in the room and in this book. I am the perfect outside observer, a part of the process with no stake in it except not to be miserable and enraged. I am the fly on the wall you always wished you could be. Let's help each other.

I see the process as it really is. I see the psychology and mind frames that color both sides of the table. I know what works and what seems like it should work but never does. I live in the middle of the aisle, I am a double agent, I'm paid by the theater or producer to help them get to know talent, but I collaborate with the actor to make us both look good. I watch hundreds of auditions a week and I get to hear the discussions that happen after. I know the way the creative staff thinks. Sometimes I'm on that staff myself. I will let you peek inside their heads and you'll never think of an audition the same way again.

There's a lot you don't know. You're a romantic. The story of the unknown who shows up off the street and lands the big Broadway lead is a good one. Reality TV bases its success on this model, and let's face it, we watch it to see the talented waitress end up with the platinum record. It's not how theater careers are made.

You're also probably a student, either at a collegiate-level training program or in subsequent private classes. From age four to twenty-one, almost an entire lifetime for thousands of actors fresh on the scene, your whole mind-set was to please the teacher, do the assignment, give the right answer, get the grade. The need for approval drives everyone, performers most of all. Unfortunately, it's the worst approach for creating art or, for that matter, for doing anything interesting in life at all.

You've also gotten stuck inside your own head. There's the pre-audition psych-up/psych-out, where you know you're *so right* for the role, you love your song, you feel in great voice, and you're loose and funny and slender and oh so pretty; then suddenly there's nothing in your book, why haven't you learned more songs, you hate your vibrato, you're way too young/old/tall/short/blond/quirky/ conventional for the role and there's no point going in except to humiliate yourself and prove once and for all that you should never have left home. But then you take the audition, and it goes fine, the big note was good, you think, maybe just okay, was it flat, were you too friendly/too talky/too jumpy/too boring/ you chose the wrong shoes/wrong song/ wrong career/why would anyone do this for a living? And then you don't get a callback and you cry, you really thought this was The One, you clearly have no sense of your own talent or lack thereof, you have nothing to offer, and you call your coach/therapist/rabbi/mom who bucks you up until you curse the blind and deaf idiots behind the table, insult the theater, the director, the reader, blame the pianist, blame the acoustics, and do everything you can to find out who got the role so you can call him/her a boring hack over margaritas with your six best friends who also didn't get a callback. All of which is profoundly unhelpful and irrelevant and certainly will not help you at the audition tomorrow morning. Rinse and repeat.

But remember, you have a partner. I have seen it all. I have heard it all. I have played it all. I remember the handful of auditions I would have been privileged to pay money to hear, and the ones that would have been rejected from *Waiting for Guffman* as too far-fetched. What you must understand, however, is that, for the most part, auditions are a numbing parade of adequate singers, well prepared and sincere, who, at the end of the day, are as polished, indistinguishable, and unmemorable as pebbles on the beach.

Why? They're thinking about the job. I'll show you how to think about your career.

2

WHAT IS AN AUDITION?
(AND WHAT IS IT NOT?)

A major regional theater is having an open call for *Guys and Dolls*. You know you'd make an amazing Adelaide, or Sarah, or Nathan, or Sky, or Big Jule, or Arvide, or Hot Box Girl, or whatever. You know to practice the famous Adelaide adenoids. You spend hundreds of dollars with your coach working on "If I Were a Bell." You know what a Sky looks like, the comic timing of a Nathan, the Hot Box smile, and if you can nail it, if you can give it to them just the way they want it, they'll have to cast you.

Then you go in, you sing like the perfect Sarah, you kick like the cutest Hot Box in the world, you nail the big note, and never hear from them again.

Here's why.

First of all, Sarah is already cast, they're only seeing Sarahs because they're required to by Actors' Equity. You're lucky it's only the one role they've cast; often it's more like half.

So, Sarahs, you're out of luck. Better hope "If I Were a Bell" is your favorite song, or you've shelled out a lot of cash for nothing.

Moving on, the Sarah they've cast is a well-known Broadway performer. She's also five foot ten. Any Skys shorter than that are off the table, says the choreographer. See ya, average-height Skys.

The director has a Bold New Take on Adelaide, and, in fact, despises the customary thick "New Yawk" accent and shrill, neurotic character voice. He wants a sexy, sultry Adelaide that will be "a revelation." Everything you Adelaides practiced was wrong.

Nathans, you almost had a chance, but except for two, you're not old enough for what the director has in mind, and you two older ones, you didn't "surprise" him.

Hot Boxes, you either danced great and didn't sing well enough, or sang great but didn't dance well enough, or sang and danced great but the music director was desperate for a high soprano and the other girl who didn't dance as well as you had the high A. Plus, the choreographer worked with her last summer and she has dance captain experience.

Et cetera, et cetera, et cetera. What is the lesson here?

You spent a lot of time trying to "put on" a character you thought was what they wanted, tried to give them the "perfect Adelaide," and it wasn't what they were looking for at all. You showed them something they didn't want, and at the same time squandered an opportunity to show them what you do best, leaving them with an impersonation of a character they've seen a thousand times. You showed them nothing of yourself and didn't give them the chance to reevaluate their own preconceptions of the role.

Let's take a deeper look inside the heads of those smiling/sullen/attentive/face-in-their-sandwich folks behind the table. The tablepeople.

You think you're nervous about this audition? What happens if you don't get this gig? You'll be disappointed, angry, depressed for a day. Then you'll go to the next audition.

What happens if the director/music director/choreographer/artistic director don't find their cast? They've sold thousands of tickets already. The show is in their subscription fliers and featured on their website. It's the big musical of the season, the one show that is guaranteed to make at least a little profit. If they don't find their Adelaide, Nathan, Sky, Hot Boxes, they are *screwed*. A bad review, no chemistry (thank you, Sky) between the leads, a schlocky Nathan, and they're losing tens, maybe hundreds of thousands of dollars in ticket sales. Theaters have gone under from one bad production in a weak economy. So you think you're nervous? Imagine what they're going through.

Then imagine just how far that turns the audition in your favor, and how much pressure that takes off of you. Think about it: the director and music director are not sitting there hoping you flub a lyric and crack on the high note. They are desperate to fall in love with every actor who walks through the door. They are hoping and praying that you're the one, they are completely on your side. They may not show it.

They may seem brusque, dismissive, depressed. This is because they spend their lives trying to fall in love dozens, hundreds of times a day and are disappointed again and again. It wears a person down. Just remember how much they need you, how much they are in your corner, how much they want you to be the answer to their casting prayers, and you'll approach the whole experience with a lot more confidence.

But the real secret is knowing what an audition really is. An audition is a business transaction. I'll say it again: *an audition is a business transaction.* No more, no less. Understand this and it will spare you a lot of heartache while freeing you to give a much better performance in, let's face it, a nerve-racking situation.

The tablepeople are in the market for goods. They need actors to fill a certain number of slots. You're an actor. You are the goods. You come in, show them what you have to offer, and they decide whether or not you have what they're looking for, *for this production.* That's it. The audition is not a referendum on your talent. It does not determine whether or not you have what it takes to be an actor. It is not even an indication of whether the tablepeople *think* you have what it takes. It is simply a way to match a market with the goods they need.

It is also not always a love-fest. Some tablepeople like jokes and chit-chat, some are all business. The former don't necessarily like you, the latter don't necessarily dislike you. You're not there to make friends, so don't be discouraged if they simply ask you to do what you came to do: show them your goods.

Taking this model a little further, there are generally two schools of thought on how to approach auditioning. Let's pretend you're selling fruit. The first strategy is to bring in a huge crate of every possible kind of fruit you can find, even if some of the fruit isn't quite ripe or just looks kind of blah. The reasoning here is that the tablepeople are bound to find *something* they can use, if presented with a wide enough variety.

The second strategy is to come in with a small, beautiful basket of only a few varieties, but each one more succulent and delicious than the next. If the quality is high enough, this school teaches, they won't be able to resist choosing you.

In my experience, the second school is by far the more useful in the long run.

First of all, there are dozens, hundreds, maybe thousands of people auditioning for the same role. If you bring in a box of average fruit, no matter how many varieties you have, the odds say that someone is more than likely to have a better one. That's just the practical side of things.

What is even more important, though, is what the quality of your fruit means to your career in general. (I promise, the fruit metaphor is almost over.) Your auditions, taken collectively, define how the industry thinks of you (or doesn't). Picture yourself a year from now, having given a hundred auditions. Think of the impression you want to have made by then, on casting agents, tablepeople, and yes, even readers and accompanists, enraged or otherwise. When they see your name on today's list, do you want the conversation to be:

"Oh, yeah, she's a pretty good belter."

"I thought she was a soprano, she sang some soprano song last time, I don't remember which."

"She does that too, a little of everything."

"Does she dance?"

"Some."

Who does that sound like? A principal? The love interest? The comic genius? Or the third chorus girl from the left? What are you trying to be?

What if, instead, the conversation went like this:

"Oh, wow, look who's coming in! I hope she does that crazy funny belt number she did last time, you'll die."

"How's her soprano?"

"Who cares? She's hysterical. I hope we can find something for her, I love her but haven't been able to use her for anything yet."

Think also of the conversation you want them to have after you leave. Choice A:

"Eh. She's okay."

"Sings pretty well. Kind of like _____ but not as funny/loud/moving/interesting."

"Who's taking lunch orders?"

Or:

"What a gorgeous and unique voice! I've never heard that song done that way, great choice. I don't know if there's anything for her in this project, but I have something next month that she'd be perfect for."

Which brings us to the second most important thing to remember: you are never just auditioning for one show. Every single person in that room is working on two or three other projects. The choreographer just got hired to do an industrial in Miami. The director has a workshop coming up and a reading of a new play at the end of the summer. Even your accompanist is music-directing a regional production and is an up-and-coming composer who will be going into the studio soon to make a demo recording.

So if you go in and give them what you think they think Adelaide sounds like, not only will you never know what that is, they're not going to think of you for all their other projects, unless one of them happens to be another *Guys and Dolls* or has a character exactly like Adelaide.

Bring your best, most ripe, most memorable fruit. Sometimes, directors don't know what they want until they see it. Or someone is so good, the director will actually change the show just to be able to cast this person. "What if we made that role a woman? Wouldn't she be fantastic?" "I never thought of that part as that type, but he showed us a whole new spin on it."

Be yourself. Two hundred percent. Bold and beautiful. In the audition room, as in life, it's the only road to success and happiness.

Now is the time, however, to remember that this is a business transaction. It is a sales pitch. Just going in and "doing your thing" is not enough. Singing Radiohead for your *Showboat* audition, although ideally suited to your voice and personality, is not helpful. It will piss off the tablepeople, no matter how rockin' you are, because it is wasting their time. There are certain requirements presented by the roles in *Showboat*, and the tablepeople must, at the very least, see whether you can fulfill them. Likewise, wearing your favorite ripped jeans and T-shirt to the *Little Women* call is not going to help them envision you as Beth.

"But wait!" you cry. "You just said to be yourself! Now you want me to be what they want to see!"

No, no, calm down, and remember, you are an actor. Although it is never a good idea to try to impersonate a narrow version of a character for an audition (or a performance, for that matter), you must acknowledge that being something of a chameleon is part of your job description. I am not asking you to put on a role like an ill-fitting costume. I am asking you to find yourself in the roles you audition for.

I am asking you to present yourself—yourself, not a character—in such a way that the tablepeople can easily picture you in the world of the show. Unless it is a very extreme world, you should have no trouble finding material that is quintessentially you, yet also in the milieu of the project. If you are auditioning for *A Little Night Music*, you need not (should not) arrive in 1903 Swedish couture and a blond wig, singing only from the score. Wear something you like that is classic, perhaps a tiny bit formal (we'll get to your clothes later, believe me) and sing a song reminiscent of the score, maybe another Sondheim, maybe not, but something that shows off who you are. I'm always hearing directors ask an actor to "sing something you really love," and am dumbstruck when the actor is unable to think of anything in his book that fits that description. Every song in your book should be an authentic joy to sing, or trust me, it will show.

In the terminology of the marketplace, you're creating a brand. What can you offer that no one else can, something that will make people remember you after you're gone? Easy: yourself. Get rid of the idea that you can figure out what they're looking for and then magically become that actor. Find yourself in the character, or at least in the world of the play, and then show them what they never knew they wanted. Average won't get you the gig. Competent won't get you a callback. People don't pay money to watch someone who is well rehearsed. They come to see personality, a unique and truthful human being who feels what they feel, only more artfully and a little more colorfully. If you can show the tablepeople that version of yourself, even if you're not right for this project, they'll remember you for the next one, and they'll have a crystal-clear picture of the quality goods you have to offer when your name comes up again.

By all means, keep training, keep adding tricks to your repertoire (I could have said "fruit to your basket" but I promised to stop that). Someone with an incredible belt who also dances pretty well is easier to cast than someone with an incredible belt and two left feet. Just be sure to concentrate on your strongest qualities first. That's how you build a brand and build a career.

3

WHAT ARE
THEY LOOKING FOR?

Although you can never know exactly what the tablepeople are looking for in any specific role, there are certain qualities and characteristics I can guarantee will move you to the top of the casting list. The first and most important, for both creative staff and audiences, is: "Is this someone I want to spend time with?" That innocuous little question has profound ramifications. Audience members have given up several hours of their evening, not to mention quite a bit of money, to spend it with a bunch of strangers on a stage. They—and therefore the tablepeople—are looking for actors who spark empathy, who make them care. They want people they can root for. For a romantic lead, it's someone they'll fall in love with; for an antagonist, someone they can love to hate.

Audiences want actors who are comfortable in their own skin, who move well and confidently, who are open and seem authentic, even though we know they're playing a role. They want to wonder, "What will happen next?" and therefore respond to actors who make it seem like anything could happen. These are ephemeral qualities, and you may be thinking, "How can I walk in a room and seem empathetic?" As Moss Hart said:

> [I]t seem[s] to me... that acting is more a fortunate quirk of the personality than it is anything else. Certainly, education, technical training and the finest Stanislavskian theories have yet to produce the same effect as an actor walking out on the stage with a curious chemistry of his own that fastens every eye in the audience upon him and fades the other actors into the scenery.

And though there is definitely something to the concept of innate "star quality," you can trust and encourage those qualities in yourself that make you, in a word, *likable*. Stage deportment, access to your emotions, an energized relaxation—these can (and should) all be taught, studied, and practiced, and can go a long way. Watching terrific actors perform will take you even further. Go and see live theater, and be an active audience member. Study your idols and your colleagues alike, ask "Why were they cast? Why do they move me? Why do I care what happens to this character?" Finding your own answers and applying them to your performances and auditions can ground you in what moves you personally as an actor and as a human being. I know, theater tickets are expensive, but watching with a critical eye is an irreplaceable learning experience. A courageous, truthful, vulnerable, passionate, or virtuoso performance can be the best acting class you ever attended and is well worth the investment.

Tablepeople, of course, need more than just charisma from their cast. Rehearsal time is not unlimited and the musical aspects of the show must at the very least be negotiated competently. Vocal range is the most obvious requirement, but things like timbre, volume, pitch, stamina, and musicianship are equally important. There's no use hiring someone who has the notes if they're shrill, tiny, flat, or poorly learned. If there is choreography, does the actor have the ability to perform it and also to learn it quickly enough? If an audition includes the reading of sides, can the actor make big choices? Any choices? Is he believable? Does he have intelligible diction?

Some directors want actors who perform a role the way it's always been done, but most of them do not, and certainly not the good ones. The majority are hoping to be surprised, to be shown a new color in a role they know very well. Though the jaded ones might say otherwise, they don't really want puppets; they want creative equals, collaborators, actors who will bring themselves to a role and make it their own. That said, they also need an actor who has the experience, training, and demeanor to take direction. Often at an audition, a director will give an actor an adjustment, any adjustment, just to see if he can make a change. It doesn't necessarily mean that's how he thinks the scene should be played, he just needs to see you work. Go with it.

Now we come to the sometimes non-PC part of casting: the type. I'm not going to argue for or against blind casting, be it with respect to race, gender, size, or any other physical characteristic. I'm simply here to report that this is an unavoidable part of the casting process. Accept it and then forget about it. You can't change your height (except minimally with shoes), you certainly can't change your race or gender. A director will either be able to see you in the world of the show or she won't. You can choose what you wear and how you do your hair and makeup, and there are smart ways to do both to increase the likelihood of a director seeing you as castable. But getting typed out is simply part of the business transaction, and there's no use railing against it.

Theater and film are visual media, and how an actor looks is part of the final artistic product. There are very conservative directors and casting agents, and there are open-minded ones, and you'll end up auditioning for both. Be informed about the project, the role(s) you might be seen for, and the director and/or casting agent. No one is just one type, of course; good actors can play a myriad of characters, and I certainly don't recommend typing yourself out of auditions too much. But unless you have unlimited free time to spend auditioning and a bottomless stomach for rejection, there's no point wasting both your time and the tablepeople's going to calls you're blatantly wrong for. Stretch your (and their) idea of what a role could look like, yes, but stay on this side of preposterous.

Technique, an empathetic quality, the ability to take direction, and a physical type that's somewhere in the ballpark: these are the top four things the tablepeople are looking for. The fifth, and it's rarely talked about in training

programs, brings us back to where we started: is this someone we want to spend time with? This time, however, I'm
talking about the weeks of rehearsals. The tablepeople are
people too, and would much rather work with someone
who is friendly, funny, smart, and eager than one who is
sullen, disengaged, bored, or defensive. Who you are in life
comes across even in the briefest of auditions. Will they
cast someone who gives a brilliant audition despite seem-
ing patronizing and standoffish? Probably. But if there's
someone else just as right who smiled and made them
laugh, who do you think will get the job? How you come
across before and after you sing/read/dance can be just as
important as your voice, acting, and *port de bras*. In this
business, a reputation for being difficult or unpleasant to
work with can be made in a day and last for years. You're
in this business presumably because you love it. Let that
show. It'll be better for everyone.

Much of the rest of this book is dedicated to giving
you the tricks, techniques, and skills to make you feel so
comfortable with the audition process that you can let
the best and most vivid parts of yourself shine through.
If you know your book is put together professionally and
how to talk to the accompanist, you'll give a looser, freer
performance. If you know your song choice presents the
strongest aspects of your voice and you've made interesting acting decisions, you'll sing better, guaranteed. If you
think about it, auditions can be the best five minutes of
your day—when else do you know for certain you'll be at
the center of attention, singing a song you love and being
100 percent yourself? It truly is your time—embrace it.

4

YOUR BOOK

Your book—the binder of songs you've brought to sing—is your reliable lifeline in the uncertain world of the audition. Lavish it with attention and it will save you again and again. A well-put-together book is how you communicate to me exactly how I should play the song you're singing and keeps me from becoming enraged. It contains all the great material you've put together that fits you like a glove, material that is organized meticulously so you can find any song in any tempo and any genre within seconds. It can make you look like a seasoned pro or like someone who's never auditioned before. It holds extra headshots, résumés, and sides (script pages) for the audition. It will keep you sane in a stressful environment, but only if you follow my rules.

THE MUSIC

Being an audition accompanist is not easy. Up to two dozen times an hour, you're handed a piece of music that you may or may not have seen before, in any key under the sun, and are expected to play it cleanly, in the right style and the right tempo, following whatever repeats and cuts the singer requests. All with maybe fifteen seconds to confer beforehand. If you or your book make my life more difficult than it already is, I will become enraged and it is your audition that will suffer. If, however, you give me music that is clearly marked and laid out, it will be smooth sailing and we can have fun.

First: all music must be in your binder. No songbooks (published scores, anthologies) are allowed—it is almost impossible to break their spines enough to guarantee that they won't close themselves and/or fall off the music rack and onto the keyboard in the middle of your audition. I can't sight-read your song and be batting pages back at the same time, and trust me, you don't want me doing that while you're performing. I won't say who, but there are pianists who will make a bigger drama of fighting books than is strictly necessary, just to pull focus and punish the singer who brought in a songbook. Xerox your music and put it in the binder.

By "binder," I mean a one- to two-inch hard binder. Floppy binders are no better than songbooks, and four-inch monster binders are incredibly unwieldy, weigh more than a small child, are impossible to find songs in, and have been known to throw themselves at me while playing and leave marks. You don't need to bring sixty songs to any audition (see chapter 7). If you really don't know what they'll ask for and want to cover all your bases, have two notebooks: a smaller one that holds the most likely candidates that sits easily on the piano, and a second that contains your full repertoire, which can live in your bag in case they ask for something unexpected. And please, make sure the rings meet exactly. Snaggle-toothed binders make page turns impossible and will end up ruining your music and my sanity.

Sleeves (plastic pockets that hold music and fit in three-ring binders): I'm not a fan. Some pianists like them because they make turning pages marginally easier; I dislike them because depending on the light in the room, they can glare terribly and obscure the music. They also make your book weigh a ton. Just take your Xeroxed pages, punch holes in them, and stick them in the binder, making sure all your music is double-sided. This is key: turning pages is an annoying fact of life for pianists, but single-sided music means I have to turn twice as many times, and I get enraged. It also means twice as many places where I have to drop one hand to turn, and twice as many opportunities to turn two pages by mistake or knock the music on the floor (I do make mistakes, which also enrages me). As a bonus, using double-sided copies keeps your book half as bulky, and saves the planet. Win-win.

There is one possible use for sleeves that I will condone. Songs three pages or less can be stored in one sleeve to protect them and then removed and spread out on the piano rack (out of the binder) when needed. Any more than three pages and you run the risk of them not fitting on the rack, so songs four pages or longer must be punched and placed in the rings. But please note: these short songs to be laid out on the piano rack must be *single-sided*, not double-sided like the ones that stay in the rings. It is surprisingly tricky to turn over a single loose page quickly while playing, and it's the fastest way for your music to get mangled. I also recommend taping these short single-sided songs together, not just because it keeps them in order, but because it makes them less likely to blow off the rack. Tape them edge to edge, that is, with no overlap of the pages. You can then fold them along the tape and fit them in your sleeve for storage.

Some singers bring in long songs taped together like this, with many pages folded along the taped hinges "accordion style." They think (or they've been told) I can turn these like a book, but they are wrong. First, they never fold flat, they're always in a puffed-up little bundle that threatens to tip or blow over. And since they're long songs, there are page turns, but these aren't single page turns, mind you— each turn is now two pages taped together. Here's the way page-turning works: to minimize the musical "hole" left by abandoning playing with one hand in order to turn a page, we pianists try to turn pages as quickly as possible and get back to playing. Trying to quickly grab a double page along a taped hinge that's attached to a bunch of other pages without missing the turn or pulling the whole song over on itself makes me extremely enraged and is a recipe for a big, distracting mess. No accordions.

When you Xerox music from songbooks to put in your binder, be very careful that you copy the *entire* page. Songbooks are generally printed on 9" x 12" paper (called "concert format"), and are therefore slightly larger than standard 8 $^1/_2$" x 11" Xerox paper. Very often, singers just stick the book in the copier without noticing the size difference, and the bottom staff of the piano part on each page gets cut off. I'm reading along and all of a sudden: no left hand. Be considerate and give me all my notes, please. When copying from a songbook, set the reduction to 93 percent; this will ensure that all my music makes it into your binder. And remember: double-sided for anything in the rings; single-sided for loose pages (three or less) to be laid out on the rack.

All songs must be in the key in which you wish to sing them. You may not ask me to transpose. This is not for my benefit, it is for yours. Transposing a potentially unfamiliar song at sight ranges from difficult to completely impossible, even for the most gifted sight-readers. It is highly likely that the pianist will be unable to do it at all, let alone well, and you will end up singing *a cappella*, or worse, with wrong chords and clusters pounding behind you. Writing in the chord names above the piano part is also unacceptable, because you never know what the pianist is going to play (see lead sheets, below). There are many options available today for acquiring songs in your key, ranging from Internet sites (often terrible, use as a last resort) to pianists and musical directors who will do it for you for a small fee. If it's a great song to add to your book, it's well worth the expense.

If you must get a song off an Internet sheet-music site, have a pianist check it before deploying it in an audition. These sites have songs stored in one key, then use a computer algorithm to transpose them to the key of your choice. These algorithms are, not surprisingly, not very nuanced in their approach to transposing and can spit out unreadable junk. There are spelling rules and conventions in music that must be followed to make a piece literate and easy to read. You may know that on a piano a G-sharp is the same note as an A-flat, but a chord spelled with the wrong one looks like gibberish, the equivalent of trying to read "Two bee oar knot too Bea." These websites should know the difference, but they often don't, so if you don't have the musical knowledge to proof a song off the Internet, please have someone do it for you.

Another bad idea, only slightly less risky than bringing in a song in the wrong key, is to bring in a lead sheet. Lead sheets are versions of songs that give only the melody line with chord names written above, often pulled from giant anthologies called fake books. Though most theater pianists can read these fairly well, the lack of a notated piano part means you never know if they'll feel the style of the song the same way you do, and you may end up having to sing your song to a shuffle beat when you'd practiced a square four, or block chords when you needed something rolling and lyrical. Most songs exist in published versions with full accompaniments. If you can't find your song, but have a recording, it's not hard to find a pianist or musical director who will transcribe it from the recording for you, though this is a tedious job and may cost you a bit more. Don't leave it to chance whether your song will be played the way you want it—get it written out.

The quality of the printed music must be high enough to be easily legible, and the pages themselves must be in good condition. This seems obvious, but I am constantly being handed third-generation faxes, smeared handwritten pages, and what appear to be failed origami projects. You'd be enraged, too. Printed music is preferable to handwritten any day, but if you can't get your hands on any other kind, check with a pianist to make sure it's clearly and correctly written. Please, no faxes—fax machines often don't have high enough resolution to re-create staff lines clearly, and sometimes automatically reduce music to make room for headers and footers. And, of course, folded, crinkled, or wadded-up music of any kind is unacceptable, even music that's just been folded in half. It looks sloppy, is insulting to your accompanist, and is guaranteed to fall off the rack.

The copy you give me must be marked with crystal clarity, again, for your sake. If I miss the cut, skip the fermata, or don't change tempo when you want me to, your audition suffers. If you're not starting at the beginning of the piano introduction, mark "START HERE" where you want to start, or use Post-its or those little colored stick-on arrows. Cuts should be marked either with brightly colored highlighter (one where I cut, another where I cut to), or some singers do a cut-and-paste job, either eliminating the cut measures entirely, or pasting blank paper over the cut measures. I should not have to turn more than one page for a cut. Repeats should be highlighted, both marks (at the beginning and the end of the repeated section). If your song has a repeat with a first and second ending and you're not doing the repeat, cross out or paste over the first ending.

Some songs have a *"D.S." or "D.S. al Coda"* marking. This means jump back to somewhere near the beginning of the song (marked with a 𝄋), play for a while, then jump forward a ways to a coda (marked with a ⊕). As you can imagine, this often leads to a page-turning nightmare. Here's what you can do: copy the entire first section of the song (the part that gets repeated) and insert it on new pages so I can just keep reading forward without flipping back. This guarantees that I won't throw the music on the floor in the middle of your song, and you will have won my everlasting gratitude.

At the end of a song, some actors write "Thank you!" or a smiley face or other doodle of affection, which causes many of us accompanists to roll our jaded eyes. Do it if you feel like it—we secretly enjoy it.

THE INDEX

Your book not only needs to hold your music, it must be organized in such a way that you know what you have and can find it by title, period, tempo, genre, or any other way that's useful to you. Here's the scenario that stops auditions cold:

> [ACTOR *sings first song.*]
>
> DIRECTOR: That was great. Do you have something else?
>
> ACTOR: Sure, what are you looking for?
> [note: this is already a mistake; the correct answer is, "Sure, I have _____ and _____," knowing that both of these are appropriate for the show]
>
> DIRECTOR: Do you have a contemporary musical theater ballad?
>
> ACTOR: Hmmm, contemporary musical theater ballad, let's see...
> [ACTOR *paws through her book, back and forth, searching desperately.*]
> I think I have... [*flip, flip*] I'm sure it's here... [*paw, paw*] I just saw it... [more pawing and flipping, while all the tablepeople are rapidly losing interest]
>
> DIRECTOR: You know what, that's fine, we have to move on.

This happens *all the time*, and as much as it makes me enraged, I also die a little for the actor who had the opportunity to sing another song and squandered it, all for lack of—tabs.

Tabs are your best friend. Do not think of going into an audition without tabs in your book, by which I mean either dividers with little colored tabs or tabs you stick directly on the pages or sleeves. These tabs hold labels for sections like "Contemporary Musical Theater Ballads" or individual song titles. When you're asked for another song, you must be able to find it *immediately*. The first page or pages of your book should be a table of contents and a list of songs by period/genre. You may arrange your book any way that makes sense to you—alphabetically by song or show, chronologically by period, etc.—but you must have some sort of index in the front. This is for those inevitable moments when you're asked for a song in a particular style and you draw a blank. Instead of the sad scene above, you can confidently turn to your index, look under "Contemporary Musical Theater Ballads" and say, "Sure, I have 'Very Unusual Way' from *Nine* or 'Whispering' from *Spring Awakening*." All your songs are tabbed, either by genre or song title, and you can turn straight to whichever song they choose with no stress, no humiliating fumbling, no wasted time. All thanks to the magic of tabs.

If you have different-length versions of the same song, say an eight-bar cut, a sixteen-bar cut, and a full version, have a different copy for each version. I don't like being told "Ignore that bright yellow highlight and the crossed-out bit here, that's for when I do the sixteen-bar cut. What I really want is to start here—no, wait, sorry, that's the eight-bar version—start here and then go to here, then turn two pages…" Forget it. Have a clean copy of each version marked specifically for each cut. These can be grouped with the full version in your book, or you may want to have a dedicated section for eight-bar and sixteen-bar cuts. There's no rule here, except to do what works cleanly and easily for you.

Having a well-organized, well-marked, and professional book takes some effort to assemble and some time to maintain and keep current, but it will make you look and feel cool, calm, and collected no matter what is asked of you in any audition. You will look like a pro, you'll be able to communicate with me efficiently and accurately, you'll make my life a whole lot easier, and I'll be able to play your song just the way you want it.

5

NUTS AND BOLTS:
EVERYTHING BUT THE SINGING

IN THE ROOM

You've got your time slot. You've prepared your material. You've signed in and are sitting in the hallway with a dozen other people, clutching binders and sipping water. Then your name is called. You:

a. jump up, barrel past the monitor, and rush into the room

b. slap on a huge grin and prepare the one-liner about current events/your trip to the audition/ your roommate/your appearance

c. grab your bag and wearily march through the door as if to a root canal

d. take a breath, smile at the monitor, and knowing you're well prepared, stride into the room ready to have fun singing the song you love that makes you sound great

I ask this obvious question because your audition starts in the hall. Your frame of mind has profound effects on your performance. If you're harried, grumpy, or hungry, it will be obvious when you walk through the door. The tablepeople want to see actors who love to perform, and I mean *love* to perform. They're stuck in that room for hours, sometimes days at a time, with fluorescent lights, stale air, often no windows, uncomfortable chairs, staring at hundreds of headshots and drinking tepid coffee. An actor who is thrilled and grateful to be performing for them and ready to have fun is like a breath of fresh air and a Venti cup of joe. Are you always going to be filled with the glowing muse of Theatre? Will the fact that you're Living Your Dream always be radiating from your every pore? Of course not. You're an actor. Fake it. You'll change the atmosphere in the room, and I guarantee you'll sing better.

For starters, pretending you love to audition takes the pressure off the eventual outcome. You have no control over whether they hire you in the end; their decision depends on a combination of factors, many of which have nothing to do with your performance at the audition. But if your goal is simply to have a ball doing what you love, if you're well prepared and singing a song that touches your soul, who has the power to make that an unpleasant experience? So they don't laugh. So they don't make eye contact. So they cut you off. So the pianist sucks. Remember that auditioning for a professional musical theater production is something relatively few people are ever privileged enough to experience and that performing for anyone, anywhere is a gift to be cherished. If any part of that sentence caused you to roll your eyes, get out of this business. Today. Even with that kind of idealism, this career can break you; without it, you're headed for a miserable life.

Your attitude is golden and you're ready to perform. What now? This is when you remember that you're taking part in a business transaction. This isn't a party or a high school reunion, it's not a therapy session or a concert at your church. It's business. The tablepeople need goods. You have goods. They have a lot of people to see in very little time. Be respectful of the transaction and of their time, starting with: don't shake hands. Seriously. They're already behind schedule, I guarantee it, and they need to hear you sing. Walk in, smile, say hello, *maybe* a "How are you?" but only if you have to. Ask them if they have a picture and résumé and if they need another. It's a simple, businesslike question that will put you at ease in the room and demonstrate your professionalism. Always have five extra headshots and résumés in your book. Always. Often, all the casting agent has is a faxed copy your agent sent (if you have an agent), which usually looks about as good as if you'd Xeroxed your face.

Next, head to the piano. If you're not sure, ask how long a cut they want. Hopefully, you know the show you're auditioning for and are confident you've selected an appropriate song. If it's a new show and you want to be absolutely sure, you can say, "It said in the breakdown you wanted a [insert style] song, I've brought [insert your song]. Is that all right?" Never ask, "So, what are you looking for?" Have something chosen and ready to go. Give your music to the accompanist and sing the song (chapters 6–9, don't worry).

Don't be in a hurry to leave. It's your audition—own it. Finish the song with confidence and don't break character until it's really and truly over. It's very easy for your mind to start evaluating the performance you just gave even while I'm playing the last few chords, and it shows on your face. How you stop performing is part of the performance. Hold the final expression for just a moment after I'm through, then drop it lightly. Don't immediately turn to me and grab your book. Most of the time, it will be crystal clear if the tablepeople want you to stay. They're experts at saying "Thank you" and meaning "We don't need to hear anything else." Or they'll just nod and you'll know that's all they need today. Accept that and understand that it doesn't necessarily mean they don't like you; they may have just heard enough to know they'll be calling you back. Asking "Don't you want to hear another song?" just makes you seem pathetic. If the first song was truly a shambles, you *might* venture "I've also prepared _____," but use this sparingly, and exit quickly and graciously if they decline.

If they do want another song, or seem unsure, have at least two additional songs prepared and ready to suggest. When they say, "Do you have something else?" your answer should be, "Absolutely, I have _____ or _____," not "Sure, what do you want to hear?" If they reject your two choices, your book will be organized so that you can immediately find what they're looking for (see chapter 4).

The pace of your audition is more important than you might realize, so I'll dwell on it a moment longer. At any call, you will probably be nervous, which, as we all know, mysteriously makes time expand. You think you're talking/walking/breathing normally, and what everyone else in the room sees is the Tasmanian Devil. On top of nerves, it's very easy for actors to take on the pace of the call itself, especially if it's an EPA or other sixteen-bar in-and-out audition. The monitor is trying to move things along, there's a general sense of frantic lateness and impatience in the room, and in an effort to please, you'll want to hurry it up for everyone. Don't. On the surface, they want you to get in and get out, but what they really want is a terrific, confident, surprising performance, which you can't give them if you're going a mile a minute. Ignore the time pressure you feel coming at you. Don't waste their time, have your book ready, don't make chitchat, but when you're ready to sing, take a second and collect yourself. It's the only way you'll give your best performance, and you'll stand out from the other crazed singers rushing through their song. If you seem like you're in a hurry to get through your song and leave, the tablepeople will be glad to let you go.

This holds true when it's clear your audition is finished. You'll either be happy with how it went or not—either way, the instinct is to rush out, and you will leave your book, your water, and your bag behind and then be That Girl who has to sheepishly intrude on the next person's audition. It's sloppy and unprofessional and not the last impression you want to leave. Take a breath, smile, say "Thank you," and leave the business transaction like a pro, all your belongings in hand. If you do forget something, ask the monitor to retrieve it for you after the next actor is through.

BEFORE YOU ARRIVE

Like any business meeting, you must be prepared in order to make the most of it and appear competent. First and foremost, know the show(s) they're casting. Unless it's a new show, be familiar with the score, listen to the cast album, and do an Internet search of actors who have played the role recently. You'll go in knowing the tone, style, and musical period, and it will help you choose your audition material. Then, find out everything you can about the theater and the show(s) you're auditioning for. Who is directing? What has he done recently? Do you have any friends who've worked for him? What can they tell you about him? Are they actually friends of his, enough to use as chitchat? It's always nice to create a little personal connection, as in "Steven Smith says hi, he's one of my best friends." Use this, however, only if you're 100 percent sure the director will remember Steven Smith, and keep it short. This strategy can also be used with the choreographer and music director. Keep a notebook of people for whom you've auditioned in the past, and ask for the pianist's card if she's good.

Don't leave promotional material behind. If you're currently in a show and it hasn't yet made it on to your résumé, hand-write it in. That will be enough to call their attention to it, there's no need to distribute postcards, or, God forbid, reviews (it happens). Likewise, if you've done the show before, don't bring clippings or pictures of yourself in the role, it invariably comes across as amateurish and desperate. The one exception would be a drag role or something else that would require a huge transformation; pictures of yourself from that production could make for an amusing (but brief) show-and-tell.

THE ULTIMATE MYSTERY: WHAT DO I WEAR?

Okay, people, it's really not that hard. The tablepeople need to see what you look like in something that's not completely removed from the world of the show. You want to wear something flattering that shows your personality. There's plenty of room to meet in the middle. For all but the most contemporary shows, your baseline outfit should be something you might wear to a nice-ish party. Men have it easy: good pants and a button-down shirt in a great color is almost always appropriate. Women, that usually means a skirt—choreographers (and directors) like to see your legs, and skirts are generally more fun than pants, though not always. You should know what colors are good for you; if you don't, ask a stylish friend to help you. Block colors or simple, small prints or stripes are best. We should be looking at you, not your houndstooth blouse or the giant camellia on your skirt. That goes for big, distracting jewelry, too—your accessories shouldn't be singing louder than you are. Too conservative can also be a problem. A blah dress makes you look blah. Men in the ubiquitous chinos and French blue shirt make me feel like I'm at Kinko's. Let your clothes reflect your personality; just don't let them outshine it.

Reject any all-black outfits. My subjective opinion is that these suck all the energy out of the room and make it seem like you just came from a funeral, but the objective fact is that you'll often be performing against a black wall or black curtains pulled across mirrors, and your body will disappear and you'll look like a floating head. The only exception is for women who absolutely *must* wear that perfect little black dress, but even then, accessorize with colored jewelry. A little visual pop adds more than you can imagine.

Avoid the temptation to wear anything too over-the-top fabulous. If we're spending all our attention on your unbelievable shoes, we're not listening to your performance. A great dress or shirt is wonderful, but keep it one notch down from Oh-My-God-Where-Did-She-Get-That? Men, I find jewelry of any kind distracting, the major culprit being huge, chunky watches. They pull focus, bounce around when you move, and I've seen them fall off more than once. Leave them in your bag. Women, avoid any jewelry that makes noise, like jingly earrings or clattering bracelets—you may be used to them, but they annoy the rest of us.

Be cautious of straying too far in formality from this model. Women, anything that might be termed a "gown" is most likely too fancy; you're not in a wedding party or going to the prom. Chiffon, crinolines, tulle or shiny satin read very costumey and should be avoided, unless you have that kind of huge personality and can wear them with an ironic wink. Slightly longer or fuller skirts might be a good choice for period shows, but nothing below the calf. Men, adding a tie can be fun, or a blazer, as long as it doesn't seem too corporate. If it's a period piece, a vest can be a good choice, just be careful it doesn't push you into "dapper," which, unless you're auditioning for *She Loves Me*, is rarely appropriate. On the other end of the spectrum, I find jeans and T-shirts too casual, except for very contemporary shows, when they are sometimes acceptable. If you think jeans are in the world of the show, make them nice jeans, nothing faded or ripped. You want to appear like the audition is a special occasion, not a trip to the bodega. Flip-flops are never acceptable; they're just too casual and, worse, unflattering. Sweat clothes look terrible on everyone.

Make sure your clothes fit. Baggy clothes do not make you look skinny, they make you look sloppy. Pants should not have to be rolled up, the shoulders of your shirts and jackets should line up with your actual shoulders. The tablepeople need to be able to see what your body really looks like. Note, however, that this doesn't mean they want to see every crease and bulge of your physique—men, you're not going to a club, and women, cleavage falls under the "too distracting" category. Sexy can be great at an audition, but leave something to the imagination.

The same guidelines apply to makeup as to clothes. Something light, a little more than everyday but not too much. We want to see your pretty face, not the pretty face you purchased at MAC. A touch more color and eye than you might wear to a party, to compensate for the likely flat and unflattering lighting, but not a full stage beat, no false eyelashes or heavy foundation. The tablepeople are just too close and it's impossible to see who you are under a mask. The only exception is if the audition is on stage in a large theater—then you may pull out your whole bag of tricks.

The traditional wisdom about wearing the same thing to the callback as you did to the first call is smart. That goes for dance calls, too. Be the Girl in the Pink Top from the beginning of the audition process to the end. The tablepeople see so many pretty girls and well-put-together guys, anything you can do to help them remember you is much appreciated.

Remember that your audition is not just what happens while the music is playing—it's the entire package you present to the tablepeople. An actor who is relaxed, cheerful, professional, and genuinely excited to perform will wake up the deadest room and put everyone at ease.

Who wouldn't want to have that kind of energy around? Complete the picture by wearing flattering clothes that show your personality without pulling focus from your performance, and you'll feel, act, and look better than most of your competition.

6

HOW TO TALK TO ME

Setting the tone with me right off the bat is crucial to having a good relationship. Many of the guidelines about speaking to the tablepeople apply to speaking with me as well. This is a business transaction; we have a business relationship. It should, of course, be cordial, but we are not friends. Even when a friend of mine appears at an audition, we don't act like we're seeing each other at a party—we get down to business.

Say hello. No handshaking, ever. I play for up to two hundred people a day, can you imagine how many colds I'd catch if I had to touch them all? And please don't take this personally, but I also don't need to know what your name is, and I don't feel like introducing myself two hundred times a day, so don't ask me mine. I'm a friendly guy, but now is not the time. I will not play better for you because I know your name, and any time spent in niceties is time we keep the tablepeople waiting. If you really like my playing, get my name afterwards, ask for my card, or get my name from the monitor. Keep things pleasant, efficient, and businesslike. Remember, though, you don't have to be in a rush. If I hear "This-is-'Don'tRainonMyParade'-we're-starting-here-no-first-ending-cut-to-here-watch-the-fermata-skip-the-last-three-bars-wait-for-my-nod-okay-thanks," I will just make you start all over again at a human pace.

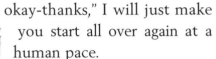

Set your music on the rack, turned to the song you're singing. Don't hand it to me so I can do it for you. Say the name of the song, to orient me. Figuring out a song's tempo, style, and feel is obviously easier if I'm already familiar with it, and when a cut starts on page 2 or 3 with no title page, it can be hard to tell what the song is. Next, point out any cuts and repeats. If a repeat is marked, with or without first and second endings, tell me whether you're taking it or not. All this should be clearly marked, of course (see chapter 4). Point out any freedoms you take with tempo: fermatas, pauses, tempo changes, etc. Important dynamic markings are also fair game, just don't go overboard—if it's marked, I should do it anyway, without your telling me. Feel free, though, if it's something dramatic or vital to your performance.

You must give a tempo, even if the pianist doesn't ask. "The usual tempo," "Kind of medium," or "Fast" are unacceptable, as they mean different things to different people. Don't leave any part of your audition to chance or interpretation. "Quarter note equals 108" may seem very specific, but I am not a metronome and can't pull that out of my head. There is only one foolproof way to make sure the accompanist plays the tempo you want: sing the first couple bars. Do this quietly, the tablepeople don't need to hear you start your song twice. Beware: this is not as easy as it sounds, and is something you will need to practice. You will be nervous and will naturally give a faster tempo than you really want. Also, many songs start with whole notes or lots of rests in the vocal line, and it can be hard to sing *a cappella* in a strict tempo. Feel free to sing the piano introduction if it's easier. You may also tap your finger or even conduct (subtly) if it helps you. This is a crucial moment in your audition—make sure you prepare this with your coach or another pianist so you can confidently give the tempo you need.

Sometimes, even with everyone's best efforts, an accompanist will take a tempo that is unworkable for you. Don't start waving or snapping in the new tempo to try to correct things. Simply and politely stop the pianist, and say, "I'm sorry, I must have given you the wrong tempo." Go back to the piano and give it again. If it was your fault, it's a classy way to handle your mistake. If the pianist was at fault, the tablepeople most likely know this and will appreciate your professionalism. Occasionally, you will encounter a grumpy accompanist (or as I like to call some of my colleagues, "pre-enraged") who will snarl, "I know how it goes!" if you try to set a tempo for a popular song. Ignore them. They don't know if you take it unusually briskly or slowly and you have a right to dictate exactly the tempo you want. Don't be intimidated by an accompanist; if you're prepared and professional, it's our job to treat you with respect.

You are responsible for knowing what you want me to play for an introduction as well as at the end of the song. Every call, singers come in who clearly have never heard the piano introduction. This means they don't know if it's way too long, how they get their note, or anything about what they'll hear right before they sing, when they're the most nervous. That is no way to feel prepared for your audition. If I see an eight-bar piano intro, I will ask where you want me to start, because unless the tempo is very fast, a two-bar intro should be plenty for any song. Work it out with a pianist beforehand so you know what to tell me and you know exactly what you'll hear to get you started.

I strongly recommend you have at least a one-bar piano intro. Starting cold (without an introduction) is an abrupt and awkward way to get into a song—I feel like a sprinter waiting for the gun to go off, and then have to catch you and catch your tempo simultaneously while getting this new song in my fingers. Even the shortest of introductions allows me to hear the feel of the song in my head and start confidently when I'm ready, giving you a smooth and polished entrance. In addition, you don't have to get your note from a bell tone or have me give it to you at the piano and then try to remember it as you walk to your place in the room. That short intro also gives the tablepeople a chance to focus their attention on you and sets the mood of the song. If you feel you absolutely have to start a song cold, rehearse it with a pianist. You need to give a strong breath or head upbeat just before you sing so I can catch you without lurching into the song. You don't have to look at me, but you do need to give some sign that you're about to sing, or we'll both spend the first couple measures getting ourselves in sync.

You must be just as organized about how you end your song. Many songs have long playoffs at the end that are unsuitable for audition purposes. You don't want to sing your big last note and then have to stand there with egg on your face listening to me dribble on. Write out a cut so I don't play more than a measure after you're done. If you're doing a cut version of a song and you're stopping in the middle, work out (or have someone write) an ending for me that feels final. It doesn't have to be great, but that whiplash feeling that occurs when someone just stops a song in the middle is not a polished or effective way to end your audition.

Once you're confident I know what you want, there's the sometimes awkward transition into starting the song. Step away from the piano and into the center of the room, not too close to the tablepeople, but not too far away. Many tablepeople like to write down what each actor sings to help remember them during deliberations, so say the title of your song. But please, speak like a human being who's actually talking to other human beings. There is a certain robotic way of doing this that I hear a lot and it's very High-School-All-County-Voice-Finals: "Hi, my name is Amber Brown and I will be singing for you today "Buddy Beware" from *Anything Goes* by Cole Porter." It sounds memorized and animatronic, and there's not a person in the room who doesn't know who wrote "Buddy Beware" and what show it's from. Remember, this audition is all about showing who you are, so just be yourself. All you need to say is "I'm doing a cut of 'Buddy Beware,'" or even just a smile and say, "This is 'Buddy Beware.'" Really. That's it. Be relaxed, be friendly, be natural.

There are different ways of letting me know when you're ready to start singing, but there are two that seem to work the best. One is the simple "I'll nod when I'm ready." If you're comfortable with that, fine, it's good for me. Sometimes, however, especially if you're singing something dramatic, you don't want to get into character, then have to break it to cue me and then get back into character. In that case, you can simply say, "I'll begin with my head slightly down, and when I raise it, please begin." That way you can stay in character and keep your focus, and I have a clear cue to start playing.

Here's how a professional pre-song conference might go:

> ACTOR: [*smiles to accompanist and sets book on piano rack, open to her song*] Hi there. This is "Buddy Beware" from *Anything Goes*. I'm starting from the top, but cut these two bars of intro [*bars are crossed out in score*] and start here. I'll go straight through, taking the second ending [*first ending is crossed out*]. I take a little breath here, take some time here, and I do this fermata, so just watch me. I end really loud, so I'd love

a big finish. Tempo is [*sings quietly and counts to fill in big rests*] "Buddy beware—two, three, four, five—buddy better take care—two, three, four, five." I'll nod when I'm ready. Thanks. [*crosses to center of room, waits till the tablepeople are done shuffling papers, smiles*] Hi. This is "Buddy Beware." [*nods pleasantly to pianist*]

It's simple, it's clean, it's efficient. It's a business transaction. It's not the Most Important Five Minutes of Your Life. You're a professional and you're dealing with other professionals in an ordinary business situation. Approach it with this attitude and you'll stay relaxed, you'll take the pressure off yourself, and you'll give a freer, more authentic performance. Your goal is always to show your true self, and no one can see you behind an aura of life-and-death terror or a polished, robotic veneer. This is probably not your first audition, nor will it be your last. Being thoroughly prepared will allow you to have as much fun as possible and will make this career a whole lot easier.

7

THE SONG

Everything I've talked about so far is important, of course, both for the impression you make to everyone in the room and for maintaining your cool and sense of fun in the audition environment. But we all know the biggest factor in whether you get a callback: *the Song*. The Song is what you've been practicing, in and out of school, for, I would safely guess, years. The Song is what makes your stomach churn, maybe even as you're reading this, what preoccupies your waking and possibly sleeping hours, what you've paid countless professionals thousands of dollars to help you select and craft and perfect. You agonize over the choice of the Song, how to frame it, interpret it, cut it, "inhabit" it or any other actory verbs of your choice. The rest of your audition is about learning the customs and accepted procedures of the room. The Song is all you.

Let's go back to why you're there. You have goods, the tablepeople are in the market for goods. The Song is how you present your goods in the best light. These goods include your voice (tone, pitch, size), your personality, and your physical appearance and bearing. You don't need to show every trick in your book. It's impossible and unhelpful, as half of your tricks are irrelevant to the role for which you're auditioning. Do your homework and know the show and role(s) for which you're being considered. Then tailor your song(s) to showcase those aspects of what you do that are most appropriate to the show, and that will most easily allow the tablepeople to picture you in their production.

Unless you intend on only auditioning for shows from one particular style and period (a bad idea), you will need a variety of material in your book. Many coaches and voice teachers have lists of "Songs You Should Have," and the ones I've seen are mostly good. Here's mine:

- **Two to four musical comedy standards**

This means anything by George Gershwin, Cole Porter, Rodgers and Hammerstein, Rodgers and Hart, Harold Arlen, E. Y. Harburg, Johnny Mercer, Irving Berlin, or Frank Loesser. You can also find similar songs by lesser-known writers (there are some gems from movies from the '30s and '40s), but these are your main guys. Try to find ones that aren't done all the time. This goes for all categories, but it's easier with this period because the canon is so vast. Sometimes an obscure Berlin or Porter song is obscure for a reason (it's dated, silly, or boring—sorry, Irv, sorry, Cole). But there are plenty of good ones that are lesser-known that will show off your tone, line, and musical phrasing without the risk of triggering a director's song allergy.

Song allergies afflict everyone, for several reasons. First, some tablepeople just get sick of songs. They almost seem to enjoy rejecting a song (or an actor) because of some allegedly uncontrollable visceral reaction. You can try to ask around, keep an ear to the ground, and avoid the song *du jour* that everyone is doing, but ultimately you have no control over a director's song allergies. You can and should, however, have a second choice prepared, just in case someone says, "Oh, God, not that again." Song allergies also occur because after hearing a song a hundred times, it becomes difficult to concentrate on the performer, no matter how much you like the song or him. It's the old law of diminishing returns: the first glass of lemonade on a hot summer day is wonderful, the tenth makes you sick. The overdone song goes by in a familiar blur, and the second you leave (or even before), they've confused you with the other four people who sang it this afternoon. People also tend to have strong opinions about extremely popular songs and how they should be interpreted, or they have certain favorite performances in their minds that you simply can't compete with. It's much easier to get a clear impression of an actor who sings a lesser-known song, one without attached baggage.

- **Two comedy songs—one old, one new**

This one is hard. Most comedy songs that have been around for more than five minutes have been done to death and are no longer funny. Tom Lehrer songs are almost impossible—we've just heard them too many times. Ditto the handful of start-off-sweet-then-turn-very-rude songs. Most importantly, don't rely on the song to be funny. "I'm Not Wearing Underwear Today" from *Avenue Q* is surprising in the show and always gets a laugh, but in an audition, simply selecting that song to sing is not enough—you must be funny yourself; you must bring your own creativity and sense of humor to the song and make it your own brand of funny.

A great strategy can be to take a song that wasn't originally a comedy song and change the context or performance to turn it on its head. One actress I know of sings "What Did I Have That I Don't Have?," a serious song, but loses a false eyelash almost immediately. She spends the rest of the song discreetly chasing it around her face while everyone in the room howls. Some actors rewrite lyrics, which can be a great idea, but do this only if you know your lyrics are funny. Try them out for honest people (not just your friends). Setting a song in a new and funny context can also work well—"He Touched Me" as a germ-phobic subway rider instead of a love song, for example. Show your creativity *and* make them laugh—it's a one-two punch that's sure to succeed. It takes extra work, but it's worth it.

- **A song that shows off your highest good notes**

For obvious reasons, high notes are generally the limiting factor when casting certain roles. An actor either has the range to sing the role or he doesn't. The most important word of this category, however, is "good." Sounding fantastic on a G is a lot better than sounding pinched and strained on a B. This is a touchy subject and one that easily leads singers to attempt unnecessary vocal feats that are beyond their ability. For some reason, this especially afflicts sopranos, so let me be specific.

Sopranos, please hear me when I tell you that your high C is not good. In fifteen years of playing auditions, I have heard two high C's that were actually terrific, and those singers both graduated from Juilliard opera. It's just not something that normal people can do brilliantly. But here's the good news: you don't have to! No one cares if you have a high C; in musical theater, there are very few roles that call for even an A. There is just no reason to put yourself and others through the trauma of trying anything higher. "A Call from the Vatican," which has a trick C at the end, is not a good audition song, and wouldn't be even if five thousand other people weren't doing it. Going up at the end of "I could have danced, danced, danced / All NIGHT!!" is alarming and in poor musical taste. Don't interpolate high notes into well-known songs, ever—someone at the table is going to *hate* it, I guarantee you. Find a song that shows off your relevant range without your needing to rewrite it. If you think you're being considered for an ensemble role in a classic, big-chorus show (Herman, Kern, Willson), some of which take ensemble sopranos quite high, find a song that has an actual A or B-flat written in it. If the musical director needs to hear something higher, he will vocalize you up. Note: for reasons I don't understand, a lot of people hate "Vanilla Ice Cream" from *She Loves Me*. Find something else (operettas are good places to look).

- **Two to four songs from contemporary musical theater—up-tempo and ballad**

This category includes Adam Guettel, William Finn, Jonathan Larson, Jason Robert Brown, Stephen Schwartz, Ahrens and Flaherty, and other writers from the last fifteen years. They have a pop feel around the edges and are usually in a colloquial or conversational voice but are definitely theater songs; that is, they show tons of character and often have a dramatic arc.

Use your ear and your musical taste when choosing contemporary musical theater songs by lesser-known or up-and-coming writers. While your friend the composer may have written a great song with a tightly focused, inventive hook, a rockin' groove, and a soaring melody, he may also have written one of hundreds of bland, meandering, verbose, and tune-free songs that I have to play every day. You need to capture the tablepeople's attention, and songs that take too long to get to the point, or don't have a point, or sound like fifty other songs aren't going to serve you. Supporting your friends is great, but it's your audition.

- **At least one Sondheim or similarly musically complex song**

Sondheim shows have notoriously difficult scores, and having a song that shows your musicianship and sense of pitch is a must. There are many current writers who are following in this vein, including Michael John LaChiusa, Ricky Ian Gordon, and Scott Frankel, and showing off your ear is very useful when auditioning for these composers.

- **One pop song and one rock song**

These are for new pop/rock scores as well as juke-box musicals and revues. You'll need to try some of these out with a pianist, as some songs that are amazing with a band fall completely flat with a lone upright. Endings can also be tricky with these songs, "repeat and fade" being a common technique that ends your audition on a limp note. If the song doesn't have a decent ending for the piano, get someone to write one. And try to find songs whose lyrics aren't completely idiotic. Anything at all that you can actually *act*, not just riff all over.

- **One patter song**

A fast song with a ton of words can be surprisingly useful. Sometimes these can be effectively created by taking a moderate-tempo song and doing it twice as fast (as long as you can make it make sense dramatically).

- **One dramatic acting piece**

With the number of shows in recent years about serious subject matter, you need a piece that explores some heftier dramatic territory. This does not mean melodramatic poperetta ranting-and-railing-at-the-Stars-type songs. *Les Misérables*, though an effective show, does not make for good audition material; it is both overdone and overblown. Often, an intense but quiet song can be much more effective in an audition room than pulling your hair out. Find a song that moves you deeply and perform it simply.

There are two types of songs to avoid. First, anything with a terribly difficult piano part, or that has lots of meter changes or other problems that make it impossible to perform with a pianist without a rehearsal. Maybe you'll get a pianist who knows the song or is an amazing reader, maybe you'll both happen to feel it the same way and miraculously stay together, but don't chance it. More than likely it won't go well, one of you will make a mistake and the train will come off the rails. There are hundreds of good songs out there, there's no need to choose one that is so tricky it has a greater than 50 percent chance of falling apart. If you have a very difficult song that is perfect for a particular call, find a pianist you can rehearse with and bring him to the audition. This is perfectly acceptable and the audition accompanist will be happy to take a break.

The second type of song to avoid is the obscure song with lots of dissonance. There are some very thorny Sondheim songs where certain notes in the vocal line sound "wrong" or dissonant with the piano, but everyone is familiar with these songs by now and knows that you're singing what he wrote. But if the song is both unfamiliar and extremely dissonant, no one will know whether what you're singing is really on the page or if you're just off-pitch. You don't want the tablepeople thinking, "Did she mean to sing that? Is she flat? What the heck is this crazy song anyway?" instead of listening to your performance. By all means choose challenging, new material; everyone in the room loves to hear new songs. Just make sure it's listener-friendly enough that people aren't left scratching their heads. Your audition should be all about you. Just like you don't want to wear clothes that draw focus, stay away from "songs that make them go 'huh?'"

Above all, choose songs that allow you to put your own personal stamp on them, songs with a definite point and point of view, filled with details that give you the chance to create a specific and unique performance. The title song from *Hello, Dolly!* is a fun tune, but there's no character there, nothing to play, no way to show who you are. That's what your audition is all about, and what makes choosing songs such a fun and personal process. With a book full of material that you love to perform that also covers all the bases of style, tempo, and period, you'll be ready to audition for any show—and have a blast doing it.

8

HOW TO SING IT—PART I: INTERPRETATION

I am not an acting teacher, and I certainly would not presume to be able to teach anyone how to act in a few pages. What I will do is share with you the kind of performance that makes for a good audition, and the kind of actors that interest me, move me, make me laugh, and generally get called back.

There's an old saying that "directing is X percent casting," with that number being anywhere from 75 to 90. The vast majority of American theater productions have between two and four weeks to rehearse, tech, and open a show. This is not enough time to teach someone how to act, generate empathy, get a laugh, or exude that special quality a particular role requires. Directors are looking for actors who come into the audition room with these attributes, while letting their own unique spark and creativity shine through. The tablepeople don't want actors who sound like everyone else. They are not impressed with competence. Being able to hit the notes is not going to get you the job. I've said it before, but here's where it counts: they want to see *who you are*. You. All your quirks and flaws, the parts you'd rather cover over and the parts you think only your friends love. Audiences respond to human beings, not smooth and slick facsimiles. No well-written character is perfect, because we cannot empathize with perfection. We want to see people who are imperfect, just like us, so we can put ourselves in their shoes and go on a journey with them.

The audition marketplace is tough. There are a lot of people trying to sell their goods and your competition is fierce. In my experience, no one comes into an audition and sings badly. Everyone can remember their song, sing on pitch, get the notes out. You are not going to be cast simply for being able to sing. Most people also know what their song is about and are able to pretend they are in love, or sad, or excited, or whatever the song dictates. Putting a wash of this sort of generic "acting" over your song therefore does not make you special—it puts you squarely in the middle of the pack. Are you extremely attractive? That might bump you up half a notch, but not enough to matter. Do only these things and you will not have a career.

And this, honestly, is what makes me the most enraged and is the main reason I wrote this book. Having your music Xeroxed incorrectly or songs in the wrong key is annoying, very annoying, but will it keep you from getting the role? No. Does it impoverish the state of the Theater? No. But thinking that a decent voice and a superficial reading of the text of a song is all that it takes to be an actor will probably keep you from getting the role, and it definitely impoverishes the state of the Theater. Art matters, and whether or not you would ever describe yourself as an "artist," that is, in fact, what you are or aspire to be by working in the Theater. All art is about the soul, and if yours isn't on the line every time you perform, you rob your audience of a unique glimpse into what it means to be human, and you do a disservice to the playwrights, composers, and lyricists whose voice you have volunteered to be, if only for sixteen bars in a rehearsal studio.

The bottom line is, it takes an incredible amount of psychological energy to create a vibrant performance, and most actors just aren't working hard enough. They think they are, but they're operating at about a seven and have never been told they go to eleven. I know this because I sit and watch hundreds of sevens walk through the door every day, and then suddenly in comes a ten and sets the room on fire. It really is that obvious. Seven doesn't work. Eight is dull. Nine is barely acceptable, ten works steadily and eleven is a star.

What does this mean for your audition? Every word, every note, every thought, phrase, emotion, image, gesture, and move must be made and felt with 100 percent commitment. Start with the text. In most auditions, you can tell the actor has sung the song so many times that it has lost its meaning. Or it comes across as a class assignment, where the goal is to reproduce what's on the page and please the teacher, to do it "right." This common attitude keeps the song at arm's length and gives the feeling that you're trying to re-create someone else's thoughts. These thoughts must be your own, you must believe that you're coming up with them and the music that they lie on in the moment.

Songs (good ones, at least) are moments of high stakes for a character, moments when expressing and communicating exactly what he or she thinks is of vital importance. Every word a character sings is a choice—you are choosing to say that word and not one of a dozen synonyms in order to get across this important idea, either to another character, yourself, or the universe. Know deeply why you're choosing each word and not another, and experience each word fully. Unlike spoken text, singing lets you linger on words and infuse them with layers of thought, maybe more than one thought on each word. This ability to take time and fill a phrase completely is what makes singing so magical when done with full investment, and what can make it fall so flat otherwise.

This means you must examine every single word. It is very easy, even for excellent, seasoned performers, to hit only the main words of a lyric. Lyrics are very dense, and lyricists choose their words with great care. Honor every word and mine all the meaning you can out of each one. Titles are easy to skip over, especially famous ones that have become catch phrases detached from their true meaning. "Some Enchanted Evening," "Embraceable You," "I've Got the World on a String"—these are delicious and surprising turns of phrase that are easy to take for granted because we've heard them a million times. Your character has not, and you must deliver these words as if they've never been thought or said before. Your audience will hear them as if for the first time, and trust me, it's a lot more fun that way.

Many actors think that they are expected to present and act the song exactly as it is in the show it comes from.

This is absolutely not true. Make up whatever scenario works for you to make the song personal and keep the stakes high. Sing it to a close friend or relative, to someone who really needs to hear it, to someone who scares you, it's up to you. The only thing you must not do is be bland. Your mantra should be the same as it is for writers of musical theater: any time a character bursts into song, it better damn well be *important*. This is not a license to put any crazy spin on a song; your take must still make sense with the lyric and be believable. Making bizarre choices and head-scratching line readings does not show personality, it shows a lack of taste and understanding of the material.

Let's take a look at a lyric and see how you can find every detail, keep it from getting repetitive, and avoid skipping over or taking for granted any word or phrase.

"On the Other Side of the Tracks,"
Coleman and Leigh, *Little Me*, 1962

On the other side of the tracks,
That is where I'm going to be.
On the other side
Of that great divide
Between fame and fortune and me.
Gonna put my shadows behind me,
Give my inhibitions the ax,
And tomorrow morning you'll find me
On the other side of the tracks.

The first line is a dangerous combination of a familiar expression and the title of this popular song. It makes it very easy to simply deliver the line and assume everyone knows what it means—that its familiarity and "baggage" will be enough to make it meaningful. It's not. Let's break it down. In your version of this song, is she speaking about literal train tracks? Does she live in the poor part of town that's cut off from the posh area she wants to live in by the railroad? That's one choice you could make, and it could absolutely work. The other is that she's using the phrase as a metaphor to describe the good life she's aiming for. Either way, you not only must have a vivid, specific picture of what that good life is, you must know what *this* side of the tracks means to her. If there's an "other" side, there is the side she's stuck on *now*, and both realities must be fully fleshed-out in your mind. What are her current circumstances? What is so disheartening, depressing, and difficult about her situation that she dreams of escaping it? No money? A terrible job? No future, no hope for improvement? Her world today must be as sharply detailed and felt in your mind as your own life. Spend time with your imagination in her world, make sketches, lists of objects and people in her reality, daily hardships, trials and insults she must endure. This sort of exercise is not only incredibly fun and rewarding, it will raise the stakes for the song and make your performance instantly more believable and detailed. You'll have an entire world to imagine as you're singing, and I guarantee it will show on your face and color your voice.

Next, what does she want? She quickly answers that: "fame and fortune." Here's another phrase that is easy to pass over as a cliché. Don't group them together, and don't take them for granted. "Fame" is different than "fortune."

What kind of fame is she looking for? In what context? What could fortune buy her? The difference between an okay singer and an artist is the difference between singing "fameandfortune" and "**Fame** and *Fortune*." Try it: say "fame." Go on, say it, with everything that word connotes for you. "Fame." Say it again with a couple more images. Now say "fortune." What does your imagination bring to that movie screen in your mind? "Fortune." I wager one of those words makes your eyes light up in a very different way than the other, as it would for your character. Every word is a choice, every word has its own meaning. How many nights has she spent dreaming of fame, magazine covers, her name on everyone's lips? Or imagining a queen's fortune, limousines, private jets, diamonds, a mansion for her family? These dreams must infuse both words as you sing them, even if they go by in two seconds in performance.

What is she going to do about her situation? "Gonna put my shadows behind me." What a great expression. What shadows, specifically? Dark experiences she's had in her current life? Things she's done that she's not proud of? A past she's running away from? Don't let the word "shadows" do the work for you, know explicitly what she's thinking of and let those images come into your head for a split second as the phrase goes by. The emotions—shame, anger, fear—will rise to the surface and color the whole line. "Give my inhibitions the ax"—two very specific word choices to harvest here. She has inhibitions. She's frustrated with her history of being unable to strut her stuff, or speak her mind, or chase her dream, whatever you decide. And her choice of the word "ax" is especially sharp (sorry), she's going to chop and cut out every part of herself and her current life that is standing in her way. Use that word—"ax": The image, the very sound of the word, how it feels when you say it, all correspond to her action. Enjoy it.

Next: "And tomorrow morning you'll find me / On the other side of the tracks." This plan isn't going to take months or years—*tomorrow morning* is when it will all change! Take that, world! What exactly is her plan? How long has she been waiting for it to fall into place? What kind of effort will it take and how has she prepared for it? And then she repeats the title, the catch phrase "On the other side of the tracks." Don't ever sing the same words the same way twice. Find a different color, a different emotion, or at the very least mean it more than you did the first time.

When a song seems to say the same thing or explore the same emotion or decision for its entirety, a good way of structuring your performance is to start not quite convinced and end up 100 percent committed to the idea. Maybe at the beginning of the song you're a little scared to even say the words. Maybe you're just "trying them on" to see how they sound, to see if you believe it. In the next A section, you start to feel more confident: "Yes, I think this sounds right, this feels right. I think I really do believe this is possible!" Often there's a B section or bridge that explores another related thought, and by the final section, you've made up your mind—you're ready to go out and act on this emotion, this plan, this crazy idea.

> On the other side of the tracks,
> Where the life is fancy and free,
> Gonna sit and fan
> On my fat divan
> While the butler buttles the tea.
> But for now I'm facing the fences,
> And I can't afford to relax,
> 'Cause the whole caboodle commences
> On the other side of the tracks.

Take a moment and do the same sort of work with this section as we did with the first. Here she uses an unusual word, "buttles," so enjoy coming up with that from "butler." Another fun word, "caboodle," should have tons of specific meaning for her; otherwise she wouldn't have chosen it. Uncommon words and expressions can be especially rich because they're so specific to the character, but only if you dig into them and treat them with just as much attention as common words.

> So I'm off and running
> Over the rail,
> I'm going gunning
> After the quail.
> Off and running,
> Send me my mail

To that great big world on the other side,
The great big world on the farther side,
The great big world on the other side of the tracks,
To that great big world
That'll open wide,
To the great big world
On the other side
Of the tracks.

This section seems especially repetitious, so make sure it grows and each line has a slightly different color and connotation. "Over the rail," "After the *quail*," "*Send me my mail*!!" "Great big world" needs a whopping five shadings or gradations or underlying emotions. Use your imagination: she can be scared, nervous, triumphant, giddy, amazed at her own newfound confidence, or a dozen other choices. Which ones you personally pick make the song yours and show us who you are. Not choosing any or making only one generic choice for the whole section deprives you and your audience of color, detail, and emotion—it's no fun, uninteresting, unmemorable, and won't get you a callback.

Songs are about high stakes and drama is about obstacles, in auditions just as in a performance. Know why you're singing this song right now—not yesterday, not five minutes from now, but right now. What just happened to make you sing? What will happen if you don't sing? To whom are you singing and what reaction do you expect? Do you get it? Especially in auditions, when you don't have a scene partner, it's crucial to have an imaginary scene going on in your head to keep you moving forward, wanting something, expecting a response, being surprised or elated or disappointed with the response you do get. An actor with an active inner scene taking place is easy to spot. Every moment is filled (even musical rests), emotions flash across her face in truthful and surprising ways, there's something at stake with every phrase, and we root for and care about her. Every phrase can be explored with this expectation/ response model. What do you hope will happen when you sing this line? The next line? The next? Even if it is a song that was a solo in the original show, it can be useful to imagine a scene partner who doesn't believe what you're saying or puts up some sort of obstacle:

"I Met a Girl," Styne, Comden, and Green, *Bells Are Ringing*, 1956

I met a girl, a wonderful girl.
("Oh, brother.")
She's really got a lot to recommend her for a girl!
("Here we go again.")
A fabulous creature, without any doubt,
("You've said that before.")
Hey, what am I getting so excited about?
("Good question, I bet you didn't even talk to her.")

It gives you a reason to keep singing and elevates every phrase with a clear intention and obstacle to overcome, that invisible person you need to convince. It also gives you something to think about besides "I sound froggy/Does the director hate this song?/This tempo's wrong/I saw X in the hall, he sings a lot better than I do/Here comes the G."

I've mentioned a particular roadblock many performers

run into, and I feel it is worth dwelling on for another moment: the classroom mindset. If you've ever taken a class (and most actors have taken hundreds), you've given performances designed to please people. You've sung countless songs hoping that you're doing it "right" and the teacher and your classmates will like it. This mindset has nothing to do with auditioning or actual theater performance. Trying to get a grade or compliment or job from someone is a completely external motivation and frame of reference. Your goal in an audition, as in a performance, is to relate personally and intimately to the material, to trust your instincts and show us your unique personality. If you're worried only about making people like you or getting the gig, your inner editor's voice will start screaming, "No! Don't do that, don't feel that, don't try that, they might not like it!" and you'll be left with a planned, flat, tight, and safe performance that shows nothing of yourself and bears little resemblance to an actual human being. The best actors come into an audition so well prepared and confident that they can be loose and spontaneous in the room, knowing that their understanding of the material is deep and grounded, and that no choice they make, nothing that comes to them in the spur of the moment, could possibly be "wrong." They can listen to their muse and go on whatever ride the song takes them on that day. It's a thrill to perform, and more thrilling to watch. Forget about the tablepeople, forget about the job, just do your thing, trust yourself and the song. It's what makes you special, and that's why people get cast. Your audition is your own time. You may do anything you want in your few minutes in the room. Own it.

9

HOW TO SING IT—PART II:
AUDITION TECHNIQUE

SIDES

Sometimes you may not get to choose your audition material. This is most common if you've been submitted by an agent, thereby bypassing the initial screening auditions. You will be given musical "sides," excerpts from the show, that the tablepeople want to hear you sing. These are generally big acting and vocal moments and they want to be 100 percent certain whomever they cast can nail them. Often the actors receive these sides with as little as twenty-four hours notice. Sensitive and realistic tablepeople give at most two musical sides and two or three scenes to prepare, but I hear nightmare stories of actors being asked to prep thirty or more pages of music and scenes. For shows from the canon, this is less burdensome; you can find a recording of the show and learn the songs that way, and you are likely already familiar with the story and characters. For new shows, however, this obviously is not possible.

Preparing material from the show for which you're auditioning is somewhat different than bringing in your own song. The director is obviously trying to imagine you in this production, so you must perform the song as if you were performing the role in the context of the show. Making up your own scene or a wildly new take on the song doesn't serve you here. Remember, though, that your audition is still about showing who you are, so your job is to find aspects or colors of the character that resonate with you personally. The director wants to see what choices you make with the material, how you can make it your own, and still remain in the world of the show.

Identify what you like most about the character. Is she full of energy and spunk? Is she troubled by questions about who she is? Does she stand up for what she believes in? Is she a lovable klutz? Over the course of a full rehearsal process, you would probably find many qualities that endear her to you, but for an audition, pick your favorite. One bold, specific, and fully realized choice will make a much better and more polished impression than several generic ones. It's your unique point of view on a character that will make you stand out from your competition and will make the character more vivid and real.

If it's a new show, and you have no way of finding out anything about it or the song or the character, make something up. Don't play it safe—make just as bold a choice as if you knew the show inside out. The tablepeople would much rather see a big, wrong choice than no choice. A big choice shows you have personality and creativity, which can be worked with. A bland, middle-of-the-road performance does not excite a director and will probably not get you a callback. Likewise, if you don't know the song 100 percent, pretend you do. Commit to every note even if you think it's wrong. Tablepeople know notes can be taught, but commitment and performance energy cannot. If you truly do not understand what is happening in a scene or song, you may ask the director a specific question, but keep it brief. This isn't a rehearsal, and what's important is what you bring to the character.

Many actors agonize over whether to hold the sides for the audition. The answer is always yes, even if you've memorized them cold. First, in the pressure of the audition, you may very well go up, and you should have the side there just in case. This relieves a lot of psychological pressure and allows you to relax (as much as possible). Secondly, it puts the tablepeople at ease. They don't spend the whole time worried that you're going to go up, and they can also relax and concentrate on your performance. Always hold the side—if you don't end up needing it, trust me, they will notice that you never looked at it.

TECHNIQUE AND STAGING

Your audition is not a performance. You don't have the benefit of an entire show to make your impression, so jump into a song with both feet. Specifically, this means that even though in the context of the actual show you might start a song very quietly and even stay very quiet throughout, at an audition this does not work. If your first eight bars are *pianissimo*, the tablepeople will write "small voice" and you'll spend the rest of the song convincing them otherwise, if they haven't tuned you out. You may start somewhat quietly if it's necessary for the arc of the song, but not too quietly, and you should quickly get to a more medium volume.

At the other end of the volume spectrum, "Louder is better" is generally true in auditions, but only as long as you don't sacrifice beautiful tone and color. People have to hear you from the balcony, but no one wants to leave with bleeding ears. I recently played a sixteen-bar EPA audition and was shocked at the number of shrill, strident, and yelly singers who had squeezed all the warmth and musicality out of their voices in the pursuit of volume. They didn't get called back—"She's loud," the tablepeople said, "but I don't want to listen to that for a whole show." You're trying to move people emotionally, not flatten their heads to the backs of their seats.

Pitch problems are the first thing that will lose you a callback. Even the non-musical tablepeople can hear when someone's off-pitch for just a note, and the musical director knows that a rehearsal period is too short a time to fix someone's ear. Check in with a coach on a regular basis, as pitch problems can sometimes be hard to self-diagnose. Lazy diction is the other problem that everyone can hear, so work your consonants with your coach, too. Enunciation that feels exaggerated to you is probably about right for singing, even in a small audition room. There's something about extremely clear diction that just sounds more confident and polished, in addition to being easier to understand. The less an audience has to work to understand you, the more at ease they will feel and the more they can concentrate on your character and your emotions.

As far as staging for an audition goes, the rule of thumb is "Don't just do something, stand there!" Standing still (this means hands and arms, too) and delivering a beautifully acted song will get you a callback every time. Don't make a gesture or take a step unless you *absolutely* have to. Then commit to it and let it go. I urge you not to plan "moves" in advance for specific phrases or words. They always look stilted and phony and are very distracting. If, in practicing the song, you naturally make a gesture or take a step at a certain place every time, note it, and if you feel it the same way in the same place at the audition, certainly do it. But nothing feels and looks more awkward than getting to a phrase in an audition, knowing you're "supposed" to raise your left hand here but not feeling it and doing it anyway. There is nothing wrong with standing and singing a song simply and honestly. I often see directors stop younger and more inexperienced actors after a few lines if they're gesticulating like a beauty queen and ask them to start again with no movement. The transformation is magical: suddenly they become human beings and we can concentrate on their performance.

Dancers: no choreography, please, that's what the dance call is for. Put your dance experience on your résumé; they'll see it. If it's a super flashy, dancey kind of song and you're doing an eight- or sixteen-bar preliminary screening audition, you may end with one fun move to punctuate the fact that you're a dancer, but that's it. And leave the chairs alone. Seated auditions are low energy, and the tablepeople need to see what your whole body looks like and how you carry yourself. Finally, do not make eye contact with the tablepeople during your song. I know there are differences in opinion about this, but truly, I have never worked with a director or musical director who enjoys it. They need to watch, evaluate, and take notes about your performance, and they can't do this if they have to be your scene partner. When I'm behind the table, I get very uncomfortable when actors sing love songs right to me—it's creepy and not how an audience would experience your performance anyway. Pick a spot a couple feet above the tablepeople's heads and use that as a focus. One or two subtle focus changes during a song can be effective, but again, only if you have to.

PRACTICING YOUR AUDITION

Reading about auditioning can be useful, but actually doing it is something else, and it's something you should practice as much as possible. You may think that it's impossible to re-create the nerves and high-stakes emotions that are attached to an actual audition where a job is on the line, but you can come close, and there are other ways of practicing and learning firsthand about auditioning that are equally useful.

I tell every singer I know that the best way to learn about what to do and not to do at an audition is to sit in on a call. You will learn more about your own audition technique by watching an afternoon of actors walk in and out the door than you will in six months of classes. Suddenly everything will become clear. Good and bad choices in material, clothes, acting, attitude, all are obvious within minutes, often seconds. Simply watching how people walk in the room can be a revelation. You'll think, "Do I seem that timid/apologetic/boring? Do I rush through the whole thing like I'm trying to get it over with?" Or you'll see someone confident, loose, and funny and think, "They look like they're having so much fun. I bet I'm not like that, but I could be."

Do anything you can to be able to sit in on an audition call. Find a friend who's a table person and ask if they need an assistant for the day. Get on the good side of a casting agent and volunteer to be a reader (the actor who sits in the room and reads the other parts when an auditioner is performing acting sides). Being a reader also lets you spend a day performing in front of the tablepeople, usually in a variety of roles (often of both genders!) and is a great opportunity to impress them. I've seen readers actually get offered roles at the end of an audition process, so let casting directors know that you're interested.

If you can't sit in on an actual call, make one yourself. Get a few friends together and rent a rehearsal room for an hour. They're cheap—$30 will get you a decent-size room. Then ask around and find a pianist who wouldn't mind playing, which shouldn't run you more than $50 for the hour. You can then run a mock audition for yourselves. If you have three friends, the whole thing will cost you only $20 each, and you get to see how other people audition and give and get friendly feedback. Trust me, you'll be nervous— I find performing for friends to be much more nerve-racking than for strangers. But do it all the way: set the room up like a real audition, wear something you'd wear to a real audition, enter and exit the room, practice your pleasant, businesslike demeanor, and forget you're singing for friends.

Audition classes and master classes can be very useful too. The quality of the teacher can vary, obviously, but most are good and everyone has at least something useful to offer. Take what inspires you and leave the rest. Plus, classes are helpful regardless of the teacher because you get to watch others audition and form your own opinions about what works and what doesn't. You hear songs you might not know and think, "I can do that song a lot better, I need to get a copy of that." Someone might do a slow version of a normally up-tempo song, inspiring you to do the same to one of your songs. You'll notice physical mannerisms and tics, odd focus choices, overacting, and countless other problems, which you can then look for in yourself. On top of that, you get to sing in front of people, which not only prepares you for auditioning, but isn't that why you got into this business to begin with?

The cheapest way to practice your audition is also the most unpleasant: sing your songs in front of the mirror. I know, it's horrifying, no one likes to do it, but it's the quickest way to identify your habits, the ones you don't even know you have. The other version of this exercise that's marginally more palatable is to video yourself. With the cheap new video cameras around today, this is an increasingly attractive option. Either in the mirror or watching yourself on a screen, you'll be amazed at what you do without knowing it. Pay special attention to your hands, feet, and eyes. Are your hands constantly flailing or returning to the same position in front of you? Do you make the same "I really mean it" gesture over and over? Hands should remain still until they absolutely have to express something important, then return to resting by your sides. If we're watching your hands, we're not watching your face. Feet should remain still as well: no shifting, shuffling, or wobbling allowed. And, of course, your eyes are the most expressive part of your body, so ask a lot of them. They never lie, and the instant your acting gets generic and you stop thinking of something specific, you can see it.

Be especially aware of "high-note eyes." This common affliction occurs when singers who are going along great, with life and intelligence in their eyes, get to a high note and suddenly stop their inner monologue and start thinking only of their palate and their vowel and their placement. This causes the eyes to go dead, something that's impossible to sense yourself unless you're singing in front of a mirror or watching a video of your performance, and it kills the impact of what should be the most thrilling moment of your song.

The techniques outlined in this chapter are essential for presenting yourself as a professional. The tablepeople aren't just looking for raw talent. They don't have time to teach someone how to stand, where to look, or not to clutch her skirt every time her character gets excited. They need polished, confident performers who can deliver a song, new or familiar, with strong choices and a crafted yet simple stage presence. This kind of maturity comes with experience, but observing others' performances and your own can help eliminate distracting mannerisms and habits and allow your personality to shine through.

10

HEADSHOTS AND RÉSUMÉS

These are your professional calling cards and represent you when you're not in the room. Most often, they will be left behind after an audition to remind people what you look like and what your experience and training is. Occasionally, they will be submitted through the mail or by an agent so directors and casting agents can select the actors they are interested in bringing in for a live audition. As with the rest of your audition, natural, professional, and efficient are your goals.

YOUR HEADSHOT

Headshots are a vital component of an audition. They can also be very expensive, so go into a session with a photographer knowing what you want and what a headshot needs to accomplish. Obviously it must be flattering, but this does not mean you should ask (or allow) your photographer to make you look like a movie star. You must look like your picture at your audition. If you have a hair and make-up artist fix you up for your shoot, don't let them give you a look you cannot re-create at home, or better yet, in five minutes in the hallway outside the audition room. If, after your audition, the tablepeople are going through the pile of pictures looking for you and your picture looks nothing like you, they won't find you. If they are looking through the comments they wrote on your headshot but can't put a face to the name, you want them to turn it over and say, "Oh, right, her, I liked her," not "Who is that? I wrote down that she was good but I don't remember seeing this girl." If you're using the headshot for pre-screening, and the director asks you to come in based on what you look like in your picture, she will be very irritated if you look nothing like that, as she will have wasted a precious time slot on someone she could've typed out.

There's enough competition out there, you don't also want to be competing with some impossible glamour version of yourself on your headshot. There's a particularly nasty acronym I've heard used by tablepeople, or seen them shake their heads and write on résumés: NAPAP. Not As Pretty As Picture. Don't be a NAPAP.

I find natural and friendly are the best sorts of shots. Have some personality, but nothing too wacky. You don't need to be smiling, but no bedroom eyes, and don't look like you hate your photographer. It really is all about the eyes, so get a photographer who knows how to make your eyes pop. Most headshot photographers have extensive portfolios online; spend some time and look through their work. Do all the shots look the same? Are they gimmicky? Are you looking at the lighting or the cool corrugated metal fence instead of the actor in front of it? Do these look like people you'd want to spend time with? Do they seem fun, creative, relaxed, smart? It's amazing what headshots can convey—trust your instincts and go with a photographer who can clearly and consistently get these kinds of shots from all his subjects.

You may follow the same general guidelines on what to wear for a shoot as for auditions. A pop of color is great, especially if it accentuates your eyes, as is a little texture, but nothing too distracting or busy. Studio shots are nice and simple, and the photographer can precisely control the lighting (and weather), which avoids a lot of hassle. On the other hand, going to an interesting location can add drama, but again, keep it subtle. The first thing the tablepeople should look at is *you*. Avoid contorted and unnatural positions, or anything that feels forced. Strangely turned necks, bizarre camera angles, squatting— all these just make the tablepeople wonder, "What is he doing? And how did he get there?" Trust that your personality and natural warmth are enough to sell yourself in a headshot—you don't have to try so hard.

Color headshots started to hit the market about ten years ago, mostly in LA, and have now spread to New York and are more and more the norm. Pretty much all headshots are digital now, so what you end up with are digital files, usually in different resolutions, which you can then e-mail, put up on your website, etc. Often a separate company will do any retouching and print the reproductions. In keeping with not letting a makeup artist transform you into a soap star, don't let the retouch artist over-airbrush you. You want to look like yourself on your best day, not your statue at Mme. Tussaud's.

There are two different orientations for headshots, landscape (horizontal) and portrait (vertical). Order at least one portrait shot. It's how most tablepeople flip through a pile, and for theaters who print little pictures next to bios in their programs, they're almost always in portrait orientation. Sending them a landscape shot means they have to crop it, which can lead to disappointing results. And be sure to have your name printed under your picture. This is very important for two reasons: again, when flipping through a pile of three hundred headshots, tablepeople don't like to have to keep turning them over to find out someone's name. Also, headshots are commonly hung in the lobbies of theaters for productions; if your name isn't on yours, the theater has to write it in or tape on a label, both of which look sloppy. Some reproduction companies offer "artistic" edging around shots, which usually makes them look like they were rescued from a fire. They're distracting and unattractive and serve no purpose. No border, or just a simple hairline if you must.

YOUR RÉSUMÉ

Headshots and résumés are stapled together back-to-back. The problem is that headshots are printed on 8" × 10" paper and résumés on 8½" × 11". Résumés must be trimmed down to 8" × 10". Reproduction companies will often provide this service, and with digital printing technology this has become easier and easier.

At the top of your résumé, list all your vital statistics. Include at the very least:

- name
- contact info, including a phone number, either yours or your agent's or both
- your height
- vocal type and range
- union membership (AEA, SAG, AFTRA, etc.) if any

There is now the option from most printers to have small alternate photos at the top of your résumé. These are okay, but often just look cluttered. Men, if you have shots with and without facial hair (which is useful), you may want to include your other look here. Otherwise, in my experience, these little photos are ignored.

Below your stats comes a list of shows you've been in, starting with the most recent, including year, role, show title, and theater. You may also include a director's name if you like. The easiest format to read is:

2010   Louis Pasteur, *Pasteur! the Musical,* Got Milk Productions (workshop)

2009   The Honey Pot (Piglet U/S, performed), *Pooh in Space,* KidStuff Tours, Leonard Nimoy, dir.

2009   Billy Bigelow, *Carousel*, Rumble Seat Dinner
        Theater (WV)

2008   Younger Brother, *Ragtime*, Jackson Hole College
        for the Arts

Don't list any pre-college credits, unless they were major roles in a professional theater. List musicals and plays separately from TV and film credits, and list commercials and voice-overs separately from roles.

Below credits comes training. This includes college and graduate degrees, plus a list of relevant classes and the teachers you've had, both in and out of school. This is where you list the different dance disciplines you've studied and with whom, voice and speech teachers, and other theater arts such as mask or circus work. After this come the "Special Skills." Please keep these relevant and minimally whimsical. Important skills to list include dialects, musical instruments played, sight-singing ability, *a cappella* experience, gymnastic training, and stage combat. If you have *one* stupid human trick you may list it if it's truly funny and you can do it on command. Impersonations must be eerily dead-on; anything remotely gross or disturbing is forbidden (you know who you are).

Above all, keep your résumé up to date, easy to read, and free from typos. Warning: don't rely on spell-check! Nothing will get the tablepeople snickering quicker than seeing that an actress has played Larry in *Oklahoma!* or Anita in *West Side Store*.

11

WHO ARE YOU?

Yyou are an actor who fell in love with the theater probably at an early age. Now you're a grown-up and you need a job. You have bills (many doubtless related to your theater training) and you don't want to wait tables or babysit for the rest of your life. You want to be paid to stand on a stage in a room full of strangers and sing, dance, and act. You are not alone.

You have done this before, perhaps not for money, certainly not always for money. You did *Pajama Game* in high school and learned to tap. You took voice lessons in college, and still do, when you can afford it. You've been critiqued in master classes in front of your peers. You've gotten the role you wanted, and you've been stuck in the chorus watching your roommate steal the show while you strike the bench at the end of scene four.

You see auditions as the great mystical gateway to your career, the one you feel you are destined to have. Though you know it's juvenile, you imagine getting the Big Break, meeting the director who understands your unique voice, the choreographer whose moves look great on you, the role that fits like a glove. You picture the critical raves, the nominations, and (I know you've practiced it) the acceptance speeches. If only you can make the right first impression, everything else will follow.

It is a lot of pressure to put on sixteen bars.

But you are not just an actor. You're a person, infinitely complex and fascinating. You bite your nails, are jealous of your best friend, hate avocados, once went hang gliding in Rio, secretly listen to Hootie & the Blowfish when you're depressed, and a million more delightful and utterly human qualities. These are what make you interesting and unique, to tablepeople and audience members alike. What a gift it is to be able to share these intimate nooks and crannies of yourself with others and help them not only better understand themselves but view all people with a greater sense of compassion.

It can be a dizzying leap of faith to believe that allowing the tablepeople a glimpse of that screwed-up person is the key to getting the career you want. Frankly, most people don't manage it. Or they manage it every now and then and, for various reasons I've described that are completely out of their control, they don't get a certain job and they stop trusting it. Trust, nurture, and cherish that muse, that quintessential You. The theater needs it. You need it, to keep auditions loose and fresh and fun and eliminate the pressure of trying to

guess and put on some perfect version of a
role that exists in some stranger's
head.

Is everyone who wants to
going to have a career in the
theater? No. There are too
many people competing
for too few jobs, espe-
cially jobs that pay enough to cover the bills. Who, then,
will achieve their dream of being a working actor? If
auditions are the main point of entry to this dream, who
will shine and be successful, who will win out over the
competition and have the opportunity to show their stuff
on stage? Can anyone truly predict anything in such a
crazy, crap-shoot business?

For any one show or casting call, the answer is no. There
are too many variables, too many personal preferences, too
many factors subject to just plain randomness and luck.
The most talented or "best" actor for a role doesn't always
get the job. She's under the weather, distracted by personal
problems, chose a song the director hates, comes too close
to or too far from lunch, has never worked at the theater
or with the director before and someone else has, has or
has not done the role before and the director wants the
opposite, or just has an off day. Much of this is out of your
control. Training and technique will help you sing through
a cold. Mental toughness and an ability to compartmen-
talize your personal life may help focus your mind when
auditioning seems like the least important thing in your
life. Personal discipline will get you to bed early the night

before a big call. The techniques I outline in this book will eliminate much of the guesswork in your audition. But it is, in the end, out of your hands. Accept it and do what you do best because you love doing it. At the very least, you won't be made miserable wondering if you should have done something different, or beat yourself up when you don't get a job.

Although the outcomes of individual casting calls are impossible to predict, one can generally spot the actors with that special something, the "it" factor that will, in the long run, give them a career. It's that unique spark inside, the one we all have but only a special few can let shine on command with total honesty, humor, vulnerability, and confidence. It can be cultivated, it can be encouraged and molded, but in the end, you must find it within yourself. Though it seems much is riding on your audition, it is the perfect place to set that spark free. It's your time. You can do whatever you want, be whomever you want to be. Let it all hang out. You will be rewarded.

Auditions are stressful. What I have given you is a list of techniques, strategies, and customary practices to make the experience as familiar and comfortable as possible. Understand the business nature of the transaction and act in a pleasant, businesslike way. Have a cleanly marked and organized book. Know how to talk to me to get me to play exactly how you need. Be prepared for any eventuality by having extra songs, headshots and résumés handy. Be smart about how you market your goods, in general and for specific calls, without ever losing your individuality. Commit to and prepare your material with equal parts fierce discipline and joyful abandon, honoring every word and every note with your own point of view. If you do all this, you will, at the very least, have an audition experience that is vastly more relaxed and enjoyable for everyone than 90 percent of your competition. You will be in control of your audition and can (at least momentarily) shut down the editor's voice in your head.

I leave you with two glimpses into my own life. First, I have a certain YouTube weakness that I want to share: TV blooper reels. I search for my favorite shows and can watch outtakes for hours. Aside from being hilarious, I find I learn a lot from watching terrific actors make mistakes and laugh at themselves. They forget a line, stumble, trip over their own tongue, and generally humiliate themselves, yet have the confidence and looseness to laugh it off and immediately give it another try. What do they care, you might ask, they already have the job! But the filming of a sitcom is a terribly stressful environment, with a live audience, cameras rolling, studio expenses mounting by the minute, a director and producer yelling instructions. It's much worse than a three-minute audition in a room with a few people sitting behind a table. And yet these actors don't beat themselves up, they don't lock down and just grind out a line—they go back and try something else fresh and new in the next take. This is exactly the attitude you should have at an audition: as free and sure of yourself as if you'd already landed the gig. Remember—they want to like you, they're already on your side, so what have you got to lose?

My second anecdote is about when I was given a free ticket to see Liza Minnelli perform her latest show at the Palace. I probably wouldn't have gone otherwise, I confess. I know she's an icon and all that, but the few performances I've seen of hers on TV shows or clips from benefits I haven't quite "gotten." I went in, honestly, a little worried that she didn't have the voice she used to, or the material would be dated, or the whole thing would be embarrassing. I left a drooling fan. Her voice was spectacular and got better with every number. Her commitment to every idea, word, phrase, and movement was 100 percent, whether it was a silly piece of fluff or a dramatic showstopper. Her energy and stage presence were electrifying—she defined "eleven." But what I most took away and will try to emulate as long as I perform and work with performers was the very tangible feeling she radiated that nothing bad could happen to her while she was on stage. She muffed a lyric, missed a starting note, got a little out of breath between numbers, and it was all okay. So what? She loved being there, she loved singing, so what if it wasn't perfect? No one came to see perfect. They came to see Liza, and she delivered pure, unadulterated Liza every single second.

Muffing a lyric at a three-minute audition is less forgivable than in a ninety-minute one-woman show, of course, and do your best not to. But if you are truly prepared and can find that place of sweet confidence within where you know that nothing bad can happen, your audition will be authentically you, and can't help but make the room sit up and take notice. And that's a gift for everyone.

See you at the piano.

Appendix

FOUR-BY-FOUR:
IN A NUTSHELL

GENERAL AUDITION TO-DO LIST

1. Book maintenance

   - Is all your music marked clearly? Are repeats, starting and ending points, first and second endings, and tempo changes easy to see?

   - Is your index up to date? Are you prepared to sing all the songs listed? If you've recently added or eliminated songs, is that reflected in the index?

   - Are all your tabs in place, and are all your songs filed under the correct tabs?

   - Do you have separate copies for different-length cuts of the same song?

   - Are there extra copies of headshots and résumés in the pockets?

   - Is your résumé up to date?

2. Repertoire maintenance

   - Do you have a wide variety of songs from different periods, in different tempos, from which to choose?

- Have you put in the time with the text of each song to make every one uniquely yours?

- Are you keeping an ear to the ground for songs that all your friends are doing and are sure to trigger a director's song allergy?

- Have you recently attended classes to observe others' mistakes and learn from what they do well?

- Are you actively searching out new material by attending shows and cabarets, looking for songs in iTunes, or doing research on YouTube? Are you asking friends who are songwriters to send you material they think is right for you? Are you going to the library and listening to any cast albums they have to find new songs?

3. Personal maintenance

- Do you have several different audition outfits to use for shows of different styles? Do they still fit?

- If you've recently changed your hair or other major aspect of your appearance, does your headshot still look like you? Is it time for a new one?

- Are you taking care of your physical health—getting enough sleep and exercise, not punishing your voice by smoking, excessive drinking, or going to loud clubs and bars and trying to shout over the music?

- Have you checked in with a vocal coach recently? Do you vocalize daily?

- Do you spend time thinking and talking about things other than theater? Outside interests are not only psychologically healthy, giving you perspective and distance from our crazy world of make-believe, but also make you a well-rounded human being, which all great actors must be.

4. Career maintenance

- Are you cultivating relationships with directors, choreographers, and casting agents in order to assist them in a call or act as a reader?

- Do you regularly (but not obnoxiously often) keep business contacts informed of your professional activities? Do you maintain an e-mail list specifically for business contacts?

- Are you keeping an online presence through Facebook, Twitter, or other social media sites?

- Do you have a website where people can find you, read your résumé, see pictures, and play audio or video clips?

- Do you have a YouTube channel?

- Are you attending parties and events where industry people might be? Jobs are won by seeing a director at a party and simply reminding him you exist.

THE DAY BEFORE TO-DO LIST

1. Book prep

- Do you have extra copies of headshots and résumés? Are your résumés up to date and trimmed and stapled to your headshots?

- Are the songs you intend to sing marked clearly?

- Are all your songs easily located in your binder via your index and tabs?

- Is your binder in good condition? Check specifically that it lies flat on a music rack and that the rings meet exactly.

2. Repertoire prep

- Have you researched and become familiar with the show(s) for which you're auditioning? Have you listened to the score? Have you looked up other actors who have played the role(s) you think you're up for?

- Do you have two up-tempo and two other songs that are stylistically similar to the world of the show? Have you run them today?

- Have you gone over what you need to tell me and practiced giving a tempo?

- Do you know exactly what the piano introduction sounds like for each song?

3. Personal prep
  - Is your chosen outfit clean and pressed?
  - Are you taking special care of your voice and overall health today? That means drinking water, getting a good night's sleep, taking cold preventatives, washing your hands, deploying any nasal or throat devices/rituals that you find helpful, etc.

4. Career prep
  - Have you researched the director, choreographer, and musical director to see if you know anyone who has worked with them before? This can be useful not only for brief personal chit-chat—"I'm good friends with Stephen Smith, he says hello"—but also for advice regarding their personal style, preferences, and manner.

AT THE AUDITION TO-DO LIST

1. Book check
  - Are the songs you plan to sing where they're supposed to be?
  - Are your headshots and résumés where they're supposed to be?

2. Repertoire check
   - Run through your songs in your head as you're waiting. Think about how much fun it's going to be to sing them.
   - Make sure you know what your back-up or second songs will be, if needed.

3. Personal check
   - Obviously, general personal appearance: hair, teeth, clothes.
   - Have you removed your watch and any jewelry that makes noise?
   - Breath. Seriously. Tablepeople don't always stay on their side of the table, and five seconds with a piece of gum can make all the difference.

4. Career check
   - Find out who's in the room. Know their names and their positions. If you've auditioned for any of them before (especially the casting agent), remind yourself. It may not come up in conversation, but you should make the connection before the moment arises, not try to dredge it up while you're talking.

AFTER THE CALL TO-DO LIST

1. Congratulate yourself. You prepped, studied, researched, and took the call seriously, which is all you can ask of yourself.

That being said—

2. Do a brief postmortem
   - How did I feel? Did I let my nerves get the better of me and make me rush through the call? Or did I remember to breathe and claim the time as my own?

- Were there any issues speaking with the accompanist? Did she play the song exactly as I wanted, at the tempo I wanted? If she didn't, double-check that the problem spots are marked clearly in the music. Maybe the accompanist wasn't paying attention, but maybe you could mark what you need better so the next accompanist can't miss it.

- If asked, could I find what I needed in my book? Was I ready for whatever they asked of me?

- What extraneous thoughts were buzzing in my head during the audition? How could I have quieted those voices before I began to sing?

- Did I have enough specifics in mind for every line of the song to focus my attention and get inside the character? Did certain lines feel a bit vague, like I was just getting by with a smile?

- Did I allow myself to have fun? If not, what got in my way? How can I set those thoughts aside next time until the audition is over?

3. Keep an audition journal. Write down the show and theater/production you auditioned for, what you sang, and who was in the room. It will help you remember if you ever come across any of the same people again. In a year, it might also be interesting to see what you sang for the shows you booked. Sometimes there's no pattern, but if one song consistently lands you the job, that would be nice to know.

4. Forget it. They're either in the market for what you're selling or they're not. If you've followed the guidelines in this book, you've put yourself and your goods forward in the best possible light. Move on. Do it enough and you're on your way to a career.

LYRIC PERMISSIONS

Grateful acknowledgment is made to the following
for permission to reprint lyrics.